FIVE WEEKS IN THE AMAZON

HMMEDIAHOUSE
FIVE WEEKS IN THE AMAZON

Sean Michael Hayes has been featured on VICE.com, MTV's "Life of Ryan", SiriusXM's "Jason Ellis Show," Witness-this.com, Offtrackplanet.com and more. He was born in Vancouver Canada and now likes to travel the world. Five Weeks in the Amazon is his first book.

CanadianHayes.com

FIVE WEEKS IN THE AMAZON
A backpacker's journey: life in the rainforest, Ayahuasca
and a Peruvian shaman's ancient diet

Sean Michael Hayes

HMMEDIAHOUSE
Vancouver, Canada - 2014
Cover Photo: Dean Bradshaw
Cover Design: Rory Doyle
Editor: Conor Kelley

Publisher's Cataloging-in-Publication data
Hayes, Sean Michael
Five Weeks in the Amazon : A backpacker's journey: life in the rainforest, Ayahuasca, and a Peruvian shaman's ancient diet
ISBN: 9780993978401
First Edition
Special discounts are available on quantity purchases by corporations, associations,and others. For details, contact the publisher at HMMEDIAHOUSE.COM

I have tried to recreate events, locales, and conversations from my memories of them. If I wrote this same story a hundred time it would be different each time, so this version is the truth as best as I recall, just like any true story is. Our memory itself is a work of fiction, we are constantly reflecting, self-editing, creating, and filling in the blanks to create a cohesive narrative of our life. We do this, and for us, it is becomes our truth. All fiction contains an element of the author's true self, and all non-fiction is touched by the personal elements of the author's life experience. In order to maintain anonymity, I have changed the identifying characteristics of some individuals and places in some instances.

Want to contact me? Find me online @canadianhayes or check out my website www.canadianhayes.com

for my mom

PROLOGUE

"At the beginning of the ceremony, nobody knows how the Ayahuasca will react, for them or anyone else. Even though I couldn't see anybody else in the dark room, I could sense overtones of apprehension within the group. We were sitting there and waiting for the Ayahuasca to do its magic, wrapped in the darkness of the night.

Before anything happened, enough time had passed for me to enter a state of internal calmness. I had been practicing my breathing techniques, trying to enter calm and meditative states for as long as possible during these ceremonies. I tried to observe, instead of control, my Ayahuasca experiences.

Without warning, an explosion of sound and light shook the entire house. The startling interruption made someone gasp, and I heard a quick squeal from somebody else.

The sky crackled to life. I knew at that moment why long ago people thought thunder was the sound coming from the gods fighting.

When it's that bright, and that loud, and so close it's right on top of you, there's no escaping it. I imagined Zeus hurling thunderbolts towards the Earth.

The small room became lit again and again by blasts of purple light. Thunder exploded at the same instant as the lightning flashed and I knew the storm was right on top of us. It shook the wooden house with every strike towards the Earth and I could feel the sky's energy pouring into the room.

Through the door, I could see the jungle illuminated with each white-hot flash of light. The room was still electrified and loud when the Ayahuasca began to start working. People started to vomit, Otillia started singing icaros, and the sounds became mixed together…"

CENTRAL
AMERICA

NORTH AMERICA

CARIBBEAN SEA

CARACAS
GUYANA
VENEZUELA
SURINAM
BOGOTA
COLOMBIA
FRENCH GUIANA
EQUATOR
ECUADOR
IQUITOS
BRAZIL
PACIFIC OCEAN
LIMA
PERU
LA PAZ
BOLIVIA
PARAGUAY
RIO DE JANEIRO
ATLANTIC OCEAN
CHILE
ARGENTINA
SANTIAGO
MONTEVIDEO
URUGUAY
BUENOS
AIRES
SOUTH AMERICA
FALKLAND
ISLANDS

CONTENTS

Look deep into nature,
then you will understand everything better
Albert Einstein

INTRODUCTION

Last year I wanted to kill myself. It wasn't the first time—that happened back when I was seventeen and ran away from home. I have a great family, so I didn't go too far, but I just felt so miserable I didn't know who else to blame. If only they could understand what I'm going through, I thought—but of course they couldn't understand. I didn't understand it myself. All I knew was that it didn't feel right to be alive.

When I was a teenager I fell in love with skateboarding. I was good, too—good enough to be the first Canadian to be featured on the cover of our national skateboard magazine twice in one year. Sometimes I blame myself for not pursuing my career further. Maybe I did sustain too many injuries, or I might not have been talented enough to be great, but the truth is, during my early twenties when I should have been proud and confident of my achievements, I didn't have enough energy to focus on skateboarding. I was too confused by the amount of pain I was in every day. The first doctor told me what I was going through was normal, that my depression would get better with medication. The next doctor didn't help me any more than the first, misdiagnosing me with Bipolar Disorder. I started doubting everything to do with mental health treatment.

The problem was that I never trusted the way the anti-depressants (Prozac, Wellbutrin, Zoloft) or mood stabilizers (Lithium) made me feel. If I was ever happy, I didn't know if the feeling was authentic or if it was a byproduct of taking my little "happy pill."

Feeling unsure about my future as a skateboarder, I transitioned into a managerial role within the skate world. I planned, drove, and did skateboard demonstrations with 12 other skaters across the entire country, and started feeling pretty good about myself. To help my depression, I began seeing an acupuncturist who, I guess you could say, began seeing me as well (she started it: I was just lying on the table when she climbed on top of me). I moved to California and started managing higher-profile pro skateboarders like Ryan Sheckler, Danny Way, and Paul Rodriguez. I stopped taking my meds.

When I was 24, I met the president of the Dominican Republic when I organized the first team of pro skaters to ever visit the country. We had a 30-person MTV staff filming the whole thing for Sheckler's show, Life of Ryan. The next year, I was flown first class to Tahiti. We got to stay in those fancy over-water bungalows and the president of that country flew us in his private jet to Bora Bora. That year, I made a six-figure salary.

However, by 26, I had nothing. I mean nothing. I denied that I had any mental health issues, instead blaming my unhappiness on my job, my relationships, living in Venice Beach, the traffic, the people—I blamed everything and everyone but myself. I turned to drinking more and taking drugs more often. I lost all sense of financial responsibility and never made it past living paycheck to paycheck. I was fired from my job just after Christmas that year.

I came up with an idea, though, a career no one had thought of before. I was going to become the first person to coach professional skateboarders. At first people thought it was absurd: why would skateboarders need coaches? But I believed that just like in most sports, good coaching could directly improve performance.

I had known Ryan Sheckler since we competed together in a contest called Slam City Jam, and our friendship grew when I was his team manager. After he broke his ankle in the finals of the 2009 X-Games, I told him I wanted to help him make a comeback. He hired me to coach him while he prepared, and with my help, he won the 2010 gold medal.

The next athlete I worked with, Aldrin Garcia, won the Guinness World Record for the highest Ollie. Not only did he break a record that had been untouched for 15 years, he did it after being air-lifted to the hospital with a concussion and a broken jaw two weeks earlier. I'm most proud of that one.

In 2012, Red Bull hired me to work with Ryan Decenzo, another top professional skateboarder. That year, he went into the finals for the NBC Dew Tour in second place, needing to beat Paul Rodriguez for the overall championship. Ryan won the championship, decimating Paul and every other competitor.

I was successful again, but my personal life was still a disaster. You would have thought I learned my lesson when I married a Dutch model after only knowing her for one month. But I didn't. During all the successes, and especially during the failures, I kept coming back to the feeling of wanting to die. I didn't hate my life. I hated how much it hurt to be alive.

I had stopped taking medication years before and convinced myself that if I just worked out a little more, or ate a little healthier, or found a more fulfilling job, then maybe I would be happy. But this never happened, and I was tired of waiting. Leaving everything behind to find answers and adventure, I went to the Amazon jungle to live with a shaman and figure out a way to fix myself.

Let me tell you about the trip that saved my life.

LANDING IN LIMA

CHAPTER ONE
WELCOME TO MY COUNTRY

TUESDAY, OCT. 30
9am, Angel Hostel, Miraflores district of Lima, Peru

My bags were heavy and the immigration officer scowled at me when I shifted my weight. When he asked me how long I was planning to stay in Peru, I told him five weeks. Satisfied with my response, he slammed a stamp into my passport, handed it back to me, and said, "Welcome to my country."

When I walked outside to smoke a cigarette, a police dog came and sniffed my leg, then continued to patrol the airport. I was unsure what to do next.

Luckily, standing outside an airport is one of the few social situations where being a smoker is a benefit. Rather than stress out inside, I can enjoy the opportunity to stand back from it all, leaning against the wall enjoying a fine American cigarette. I'm casual, cool, without a care in the world—at least, that's how I want to appear. Pathetic, I know.

Taxi drivers shouted English phrases to anyone who looked like me, a tourist. 'Taxi,' 'Cheap hotel,' 'Good price,' they called. In a kind yet stern way, I denied their initial offers. It would be foolish to rush into a transaction with the first driver who approached me. I made that mistake a few months earlier in Prague. It was my own fault. When I got off the plane, I assumed I could trust the taxi drivers. Halfway through our drive, I wasn't sure whether to laugh or get angry when I saw the meter spinning faster than it should have been. I ended up getting an overpriced and late-night street tour of where the hookers worked. Cute Eastern European girls, but not my thing.

I stepped away from the wall, entering the swarms of people, and felt a tinge of hesitation. *Am I excited?* I thought. *Am I nervous? Is there a difference between the two?*

"*Necessita un taxi?*" A short, smartly-dressed, and old-faced man walked up and asked me. I could only understand the word 'taxi.'

This was day one of my self-taught, "learn by doing," Spanish program. I devised this strategy to save me time and effort. I wanted to make learning Spanish more fun than when I studied French in school, so rather than waste my time with textbooks, I was going to learn by doing.

"Habblasse English?" I sputtered pathetically.

He grinned, and his coffee-colored cheeks folded into an accordion of skin. The color of his face contrasted greatly with his bright teeth and his wrinkles reminded me of the ones my dad has. You only get wrinkles like that when you've spent the better part of your life smiling.

"*No hablo Ingles, pero no es necesario,*" he said. Again, I barely understood what he said, but it was obvious I needed a ride, he had a taxi, and we just had a friendly exchange. I took the final drag off my cigarette and flicked it from between my fingers onto the curb.

"Ok," I said, and reached for my bags.

"No, no," he said as he stepped forward and pushed me aside with a gentle hand. He prepared himself to lift my big pack, the one I call "Big Red," and I stepped back. *It would have been easy for me to carry both of my bags*, I thought as he prepared himself to lift Big Red. He was so eager to help, though, I thought it would be rude to deny him.

He struggled to find his balance under the top-heavy load. The bag was close to the same height as him, and I'd bet close to the same weight as well. I watched him take a few tiny steps to steady himself, and then look back to see if I was ready to follow him. Not bad for a guy who looked over 70 years old.

We got to his taxi and I motioned that I wanted to sit next to him up front. He shrugged his shoulders, as if to say "Why not?" then opened the trunk for Big Red. I put my grey bag, "The Mothership," with my skateboard clipped on the outside, in the back seat. After clearing some papers off the passenger seat, he reached over to unlock my door.

We drove out of the airport and through downtown Lima. After making our way through the city, we hit the coast and drove south for half an hour towards the Miraflores district of the city. I planned to get some experience with the cultural barriers here before flying into the Amazon jungle on Saturday. Like a mountaineer climbing a high peak, I planned to use the tourist-friendly Miraflores zone as my Peruvian base-camp. Once acclimatized to the culture, my real adventure will be less daunting: figuring out how to get to the shaman's house.

As we pulled up to the dusty Angel Hostel, the dashboard clock showed it was almost midnight. By this point, I was just happy to be done traveling. I paid the taxi driver—more than I probably should have—and grabbed my bags.

The night had taken complete ownership over the day, but it was still damn hot. For a Canadian guy this kind of heat was exotic, and the humidity overwhelming—I liked it, though!

I piled my bags next to the iron gate underneath the hostel's green neon sign. My entire body was moist. I found the buzzer hanging loosely from two wires that came out of the cracked and peeling wall. I pushed it, hoping it wouldn't shock me, and it responded with a shrill cry from down the dark hallway. I peered through the locked gate and saw a fluorescent light flicker to life. A Peruvian boy drifted out of the shadows of the dimly lit hall, and his lazy posture made him look exhausted. The sound of the buzzer must have woken him. He fumbled with the keys before unlocking the gate and pulling it inwards. I waited for the rusty hinges to stop squeaking and then extended my hand.

"Sean," I said with a smile.

"Jose," he replied and placed his small hand in mine.

Soon after that, it became clear there was a massive communication barrier. I realized that, just like with my taxi driver, Jose and I weren't going to be able to understand each other. I reflected on this fact as he led me down the clay-tiled hallway, and it dawned on me that this inability to communicate was going to be a consistent challenge here in Peru.

Jose sat down behind a wooden table that served as both reception desk and information kiosk. I helped him locate my name on the worn ledger, which lay between us, and paused to give him a closer look. Examining his oversized soccer jersey, dirty cargo shorts and knock-off Tommy Hilfiger flip-flops, I noticed that his face was young, but his eyes looked old and tired. His skin was smooth; it shone where the fluorescent lights reflected off of it. It was the ragged wrinkles in the corner of his eyes, like my taxi driver had, which made him look worn out, and much older than teenager. *How did he end up here?*

I decided to spend an extra ten dollars a night and get a private room rather than staying in the more economic dorm-style room. Jose rattled off some information about the hostel in Spanish and I nodded along with him, oblivious to whatever he said.

He handed me a well-worn key and I followed him out of the reception area and into the communal kitchen. He pointed across to a shared bathroom, then straight ahead at room #6.

The first thing I did in the room was pull out some fresh clothes and take a shower to wash off the grime of travel.

After I changed, I unclipped my skateboard from my bag, checked to make sure I had my room key, and walked out, locking my door.

The kitchen was dark and I followed the hum of the television coming from the reception area. Jose opened one eye in my direction and I made a few hokey gestures, indicating with childish body language that I wanted to go out. He peeled himself off the couch and walked with me down the hallway to unlock the gate. We said *adios* to each other and he yawned as he slid the rusty bolt back into place.

I threw my skateboard under my feet, lit a cigarette, and skated into the humid night. Most businesses were closed, but there were lots of casinos, bars, and clubs still open and busy with customers. I kept skating. There were bums sleeping, teenagers playing music, shadowy parks with no one in them, and fast-food restaurants filled with adults. I saw people laughing in the streets with their friends, drinking beers, getting in and out of taxis. It was the same general buzz that you'd find in most big cities, but everything from the cars' horns to the colors of the street graffiti was foreign and different. It felt new and exciting.

After I'd skated past some of the busier streets, I dragged my heel along the ground and brought myself to a stop outside a bar so small it only had two tables and four bar stools. Paunchy bass and melodic trumpets poured onto the street from inside, and when the female bartender winked at me I was lured in.

I was a good foot taller than the two guys I sat next to at the counter and I instantly felt self-conscious. I reached out for the cocktail menu. The drinks had flashy names like El Diablo, or Cadillac, and they all had long Spanish descriptions. I scanned the menu and recognized the word Heineken. *At least I won't embarrass myself if I order something I can pronounce*, I thought.

"Uno Heineken, poor favor," I asked the bartender when she spun towards me.

One beer turned into three or four, and the bartender tried to start a conversation with me, but it wasn't any use. The only thing I understood from her two-minute speech was that I should try a drink called a Pisco Sour. She turned and pointed to an elaborate chalk drawing that showcased the Pisco Sour shimmering in a glass filled with ice cubes that looked real enough to drink out of.

It was a perfect time of the night to try the *authentico cocktail de Peru*, as she called it. Grinning, I nodded my head to accept her offer, and watched her create the drink by hand. Cutting two limes in half, she pressed them over a shot glass until it was full. Then she poured the shot glass into a cocktail shaker and reached up for a clear bottle of liqueur. She added a shot of that, three more shots from a different bottle, and finally, a half shot of honey-colored syrup.

I thought that was it, but then she walked away from the bar and into the kitchen. She came back with an egg, cracked it, and let the egg white slide into the shaker.

She was cute and the other two guys sat up straighter than I did when she danced to the music, moving her hips and shaking the cocktail to the beat. Her hips kept moving for a moment after her hands stopped, then she stepped towards the bar and strained the drink into an old-fashioned cocktail glass. After sprinkling an auburn powder on top, she stepped back, looking satisfied.

I pushed the straw aside with my lips and placed them on the edge of the frosty cup. My first sip of the blended drink started out sweet and sugary, yet as the name would suggest, it finished with a tart, sour taste. It was strong and tasty and I took a long second sip. They were the kind of drink that would get you into trouble if you were thirsty. I was damn thirsty.

After finishing the first I ordered another. I watched the soccer highlights with the two guys at the bar—they scored, they missed, they won, they lost—and it held my attention for a few moments, but I had more fun making up stories in my mind about the Mariachi singers posing in the black-and-white photos behind the bar.

My thirst quenched, I started feeling an anxious desire to explore the city, so I paid my bill. Grabbing my skateboard, I said *adios* to the bartender and the two guys.

I jumped off the curb onto my board and skated into the night. I was rolling thunder, the sound from my wheels echoing off the cement buildings. I coasted down the middle of a deserted street and took a deep breath. I made big carving turns across both empty lanes and let the incline of the hill direct me through the city.

It was dark and the streets were empty. After a few dozen blocks, the streets began to get darker and I began to feel uneasiness in my gut. The street I had been absently following began to flatten and I slowed down. My wheels became quieter, and like an incoming tide, the foreign sights, sounds, and smells washed over me.

At a certain point, I admitted to myself that I was lost. I stopped to pick up my board. My heart began to beat faster and adrenalin flushed into my body. I felt my senses become hyper-aware. I touched my forehead and felt the humid night moist on my skin.

What a fool I was for not paying better attention to the sideways and angled streets. I wasn't just lost; I was lost and alone in a foreign city. Not only that, I couldn't communicate with anyone. Fear consumed me.

I tried to find my way back along the streets I had come down, but every street I turned down looked more and more foreign. I saw a policeman standing on a corner, and went to ask him for help. As I walked up to him, I felt relieved, but as quickly as I opened my mouth, I realized it was no use. Neither of us knew what the other one was saying and eventually he gave up, turning away and dismissing me with a wave of his hand.

The hairs on the back of my neck pulled to attention and pressed themselves against the collar of my shirt as I skated away from him. Even darker than the streets were the people huddling in unlit alleys and crouching together in small groups under shadowy doorways. They stared out at me, unblinking and destitute. Some of them whistled and shouted at me as I rolled past them.

Most of them were scrawny men with sunken eyes. On one of the corners, I passed a group of street women who offered themselves to me. I kept skating.

I continued skating along the deserted roads, *I think I passed the same building 10 minutes ago*, I thought; *did I go in a circle somehow? Where the hell am I?*

There wasn't anything else to do, the streets looked pretty dangerous and I couldn't just sit down. I had to keep going. *If I pay closer attention to each street*, I thought, *maybe I'll see a familiar landmark.*

Suddenly, I remembered I had put one of the Angel Hostel's cards in my wallet. I pulled it out and turned back, hoping to find the policeman and show him the hostel I was trying to find. I didn't see him anywhere, though. The panic inside of me started as a little voice but kept getting louder as it became clearer that I could disappear at any moment and no one would know.

I turned a corner and let out a massive exhale when I caught a glimpse of the glowing neon sign of the Angel Hostel. Relief settled inside of me when I saw Jose appear out of the dark hall to answer the buzzer.

He opened the gate and we nodded to one another without saying anything. When we got to the reception area, he broke our silence by saying, "*buenos noches.*"

The soft voice from the TV whispered soccer highlights and he curled up on the couch in front of it and closed his eyes.

I went into my room and sat down on my bed. I had the comforting feeling I always get when I make it back safely to my private room.

Somebody was shaking my shoulder violently. I was asleep on my stomach. My face was buried in the pillow, and arms wrapped around it, but for some reason Jose—whose name suddenly appeared in my mind—insisted I get up right away.

He pronounced my name like *John.* "Shon wake now!" he said. I burrowed my face a little deeper in the pillow and Jose pulled on my shoulder again.

"Shon, please, wake." Jose leaned closer and said more urgently.

"OK!" I replied as I rolled over to face him. The sun burned into the room through the skylight behind his head. I looked up at Jose's pleading face, his eyes pressing me to hurry.

I looked down to examine myself and saw all I was wearing was a pair of boxers. The sheets were peeled back and tangled, looking like someone had been wrestling—not sleeping—in them.

Jose took a step back from the bed and the sun jumped out from behind him. It slammed my head back onto the pillow and I tried to think straight: *Why is he in my room? Why does he want me to wake up so early? Is he excited to offer me breakfast?*

Squinting, I recognized that it was indeed Jose, the little Peruvian who had checked me into my room. *But why is the bed facing a different direction than the one he gave me last night? And where are all my bags?*

"Is this my room?" I asked.

Jose didn't understand me and he looked as confused as I was by what was going on. We came to an understanding that needed no language, and we both laughed at one another's confusion.

I crawled out of the bed. Walking into the communal kitchen, I saw the door to my room—#6—half-open across from me.

I tried to figure out how I had ended up half-naked in a different room, in sheets that looked so twisted they might as well have been spat out of a tornado—*Did I sleep walk? Did I go to sleep in someone else's room?*

I walked into my room and before I shut the door Jose held it open, and with his best English he pointed to my bed and said, "You sleep in you room, OK?"

"OK," I replied, and with the click of my door I put to rest day one of my South American adventure.

Besides thinking about last night, I have been contemplating whether or not to start the special Ayahuasca diet today, including the part with no sexual activity whatsoever, but I think I'll wait until tomorrow. I should be fine as long as I stick to it for a few days it before I ingest the plant medicine.

After all the communication debacles I've had so far, I don't know if I'll even be able to order breakfast this morning. There's no better time to figure it out than right now though. Coffee, here I come!

CHAPTER TWO
CULTURE CLASH

WEDNESDAY, OCTOBER 31
11am, Kennedy Park, Miraflores

All I'd wanted was breakfast. It was too early to be judged like this. The waiter had made it clear how he felt when he slowly repeated himself. Seeing that I still didn't understand him, he audibly snorted and looked at me like I was a dumb punk.

I tried my best to understand him. "*No hablas Espanol,*" I'd said. He gave me a look of disgust. It's the kind of look someone gives you when they realize you don't speak their language, and assume you're stupid. I'm not stupid–I just didn't know enough Spanish to decipher his hyper-fast slang.

I explored Miraflores by skateboard yesterday, and I'd argue it's the best form of transportation when getting to know a city. By bike, you can cover more distance. On foot, you get to look at a specific area. But you get a mix of both on a skateboard. You can get off and walk in places of interest, and travel quickly through places that aren't.

I rode my board back and forth through the city, through the busy streets. Up curbs and down stairs, crisscrossing between pedestrians, through parks, across busy plazas, past the clay courts of the tennis club, and down to where the city meets a street named *Circuito de Playa* which is lined with apartments that stand like sentries along the cliff that drops down to a beach below. The beach is sandy and swallowed by each wave from the gray-blue Pacific Ocean, which transitions on the horizon seamlessly into a pure-gray sky.

Circuito de Playa, I learned, is the road we drove in on last night from the airport along the coast. Along the cliff there is a wide cement bike path winding over and around grassy knolls.

I crossed the busy road and looked to my left, and on the hill in the distance there's a statue of Jesus that I'd seen lit up last night. In the daytime, though, he stood lifeless and unconvincing. Throwing my board down, I went right and pushed and pushed along the bike path until the tiny muscles in my feet screamed for relief.

I was about to turn back to my hostel when I saw a skatepark around the corner of the path. Rolling past the dazed security guard who was sitting in a little wooden shack, I dropped in. A couple kids were already skating and a half hour later a group of Argentinian teenagers descended on the park.

They burst into the park like a pack of bees and their excitement was contagious. The kids who were already there sat down against the chain-link fence that went along the edge of the skatepark and watched.

The Argentinians were good. I had just barely begun to warm up but the explosive enthusiasm they brought to the session quickly got my blood going. The tricks started getting more technical and some of us were flying down the handrails or charging full speed through the bowl. The place was filled with shouts and cheers. Even the security guard stood up to see what the excitement was about.

Once we found a natural pace, the hierarchy of the skate session became established. It wasn't the best skatepark in the world, the cement was a bit wavy and cracked, but it might be the best location I've ever seen.

An observer might watch a group of skaters flying around a skatepark and think it is uncontrolled chaos. But it is not. There are precise calculations taking place which have taken years of experience to learn. The more talented the skaters, the more controlled the chaos.

We skated hard for about 30 minutes and when I needed a break, I sat down with a few of the Argentinian skaters who were in Peru on summer break.

Sweat dripped off me and I looked up at the sun with a smile on my face. Even behind the pollution and the cloudy marine layer, the UV rays were strong and had been baking me while I skated.

The Argentinians chatted with me in English and told me they were traveling students on their summer break. They asked me if I wanted to smoke a joint with them. When we left the skatepark I noticed the security guard had resumed his statue-like pose in the hut.

We walked out onto the small grassy field beside the skatepark and sat down in a circle like true hippies. The kid with a ratty ponytail struggled to roll a joint and I offered to take over. He'd told me he was 15 years old, which means I've been rolling joints for as long as he's been alive.

He handed me the skateboard he'd been using as a rolling-tray and a minute later, I handed back a two-paper cone. Personally, I prefer a joint mixed with tobacco, but I've learned it is better to ask what the locals want. You make more friends that way. These guys? They wanted me to roll a joint of pure *marihuana*.

We sat on the edge of Peru and passed the joint around our little hippy circle. When the joint was finished, our conversation slowed and we drew our attention to the horizon.

The sun dipped in the sky, dove into the ocean and a cool breeze began to blow as the final sliver of sunset-orange was disappearing. The ocean sent its salty breath into the urban expanse, soothing the city like the first breath of fresh air after a busy day.

I'm glad I took my friend Kari's advice to stay here in Miraflores. While it's not all that glamorous, it seems a little nicer than downtown Lima. I like how it's perched on top of a cliff that overlooks the ocean. The busy and energized streets were a mix of historic Spanish architecture juxtaposed with sleek modern office buildings. It makes the city look like it is growing as though it really is alive.

Sounds from the city fill my ears with uncommon musical notes. Laughter sounds different, the cars honk constantly, there is no English, but at the same time I notice my senses are excited. This is why I love traveling.

When I woke up, I was sore from skating, but it felt good to get some exercise. Back home I've been so caught up with life that procrastination has become more of a habit than exercising. I'm constantly reminded of that fact today. Maybe tomorrow I'll start running. Today I'm too sore. But if I start tomorrow, and remain consistent, I'll be back in shape by the time I get home.

It's been more difficult to detach from the "Western world" than I was expecting, especially with regards to my cell phone. Since I got here, my loneliness has manifested itself several times an hour. Even though I know I don't have any cell service I'll reach into my pocket and pull my phone out thinking I have received an email or text message.

Unless I'm connected to a Wi-Fi network there's no way my phone can receive messages. Yet, I do this over and over automatically and then feel stupid. Even though my logical mind knows there is no message, my subconscious mind is searching for something that comes from a deeper issue. I recognize these feelings are unreasonable and I want to let go of whatever they are attached to. Screw my phone! I shouldn't even care what's happening back home. Not when so much is happening right in front of me.

To me, Halloween isn't a real holiday. But if it was, it would be my favorite. It's today, falling on a Wednesday this year, but in California everyone celebrated last Saturday. I loved Halloween when I was a kid because at the end of the night I'd end up with a pillowcase full of candy. Little did I know what this holiday had in store for me as an adult! Just thinking about it makes the back corners of my mouth salivate.

I went to a Halloween party in a mansion with Kelsey, the girl I'm seeing, and a bunch of our friends. It was first-class. Before the party, Kelsey and I had a half-joking (my half), and half-serious (her half), debate over which costume she should wear. She wanted to wear something "sexy." I lay on her bed and watched multiple wardrobe changes (strip teases), which led to creative brainstorming (sex), and somewhere in between she decided on the she-devil costume.

She reached down to her ankles and pulled slightly ripped fishnet stockings up her long, slender legs. Her short skirt hung like a drape off her firm ass and when she leaned towards the mirror to fix her eyeliner, it slid higher up the back of her legs. From the shadows of her hemline, I could see where her lace stockings ended and the crease at the top of her thighs became exposed. It was memories like that that make it my favorite quasi-holiday.

I'm thinking about going to see what kind of fun/trouble I can get into in Lima tonight. I don't necessarily need to find another sexy-devil, but what's the harm in looking? I'll get serious about the reason I came here tomorrow. Today, I just want to escape my problems. The darkness is overpowering. I feel like it's stalking me.

CHAPTER THREE
HALOWEEN WANTS TO KILL ME

THURSDAY, NOVEMBER 1
7:30pm, Angel Hostel

I'm sunken and I feel alone. It's not a new feeling; I've felt this way before. This is why I'm compelled to take a good look at myself. What the hell's wrong with me? I know I can't keep blaming situations, or other people for my problems. Am I tormented by some kind of karmic debt for past wrongdoings? Is there a *darkness* inside of me which needs to be released? I'm curious to find out if isolation will hurt or help me.

I have come a long way since being misdiagnosed with Bipolar Disorder six years ago. Back then, I was a sheep, blindly following doctors because I thought they were the only ones who could tend to my troubled mind. But now I see them for the fear-mongers they truly are. I believe humans are meant to live a natural and happy life, and there's no reason why a man cannot, excepting his own wrongdoings, be completely fulfilled in this.

I refused to hide behind a theory about me that came from an out-of-touch doctor. I am a human, not a sickness. I may feel the suffering all around me, but I'm not a patient and I never want to be one!

That's part of the reason I came here. No matter what I have tried I haven't been able to escape the black dog of depression that's chased me my entire adult life. I want to explore the natural remedies of the jungle because I don't trust the people who provide, and the companies that produce, prescription medications. I want to utilize what nature provides. I have found pure happiness before; I know it just as well as I know true pain. Now I want to figure out how to obtain the former and release the latter.

Maybe feeling lonely is normal when you're traveling alone? Or maybe it has to do with the fact I'm really fucking hungover and I got ripped off by a bum last night.

The first bar had rock and roll playing but the people were louder than the music, and the lights were too bright, so I went outside. On the street I stood near some people who were smoking and I sipped on my bottle of beer. It was a warm night and a lot of people were dressed up to go out, but only a few people had on Halloween costumes.

I walked down the street and a promoter handed me a ticket for free entry to the *Discotechque Mundo*. When I looked around I saw the bar was across the street. I went over and gave my ticket to the bouncer standing next to a velvet rope.

He tore my ticket in half, handed half of it back, and pulled one of the double doors open to let me past him. Inside the door was a cement hallway lit with cool-green lights leading towards another closed door. The muffled sound of electronic music rolled past me as I got closer, and when I opened the door the music hit me right in the chest.

I blinked a few times to adjust my eyes to the flashing strobe lights. In front of me was a huge open room, which on the far side was split into two levels. Downstairs was a dance floor surrounded with bars on all sides that had floor-to-ceiling mirrors behind them. Upstairs in the back, there was a balcony with tables with what looked like a more *exclusive* clientele than the level below. They were mostly men wearing nice suits with bottles of liquor in silver buckets in front of them. Some of them were schmoozing with girls that looked high maintenance and were probably high-priced.

Both floors were packed with partygoers and everyone was dressed well. I watched the crowd dancing to the high-energy house music and it was the kind of music that I couldn't help but move to. It started down in my ankles and moved up my body until I was bobbing my head. Going across the room, I tried to befriend the DJ.

He replied to me in English when I complimented him on his choice of song which was called "Can't Leave Me" by one of my favorite artists, Maceo Plex. The DJ told me he was from Ecuador and that he loved my hometown of Vancouver, Canada.

In the middle of one of the songs, the DJ took off his headphones and invited me to join his friends that were sitting at a small table behind him.

As I stepped up onto the tiny stage and past his laptop and DJ gear, I looked out at the crowd. Neon lights bounced across the dance floor, illuminating well-dressed men with their flashy female counterparts. The music was loud, and the crowd responded to its beat like they were a singular organism.

When I sat down with the DJ's friends, we did our best to understand each other, but it was pretty hard because the music was loud and none of them spoke English. I couldn't understand much when they talked amongst themselves, but it was still fun to hang out with some new friends in a foreign country. The language barrier didn't matter because we were smiling, we had comfortable body language, and I was drunk.

A cute waitress came up to the edge of the stage and asked if we wanted to order anything. I circled my hand around the table, to include my new friends, and ordered a round of *Cusquena* beers. Besides skateboarding, buying a round of drinks is a great way to get accepted by the locals anywhere in the world. When in doubt, buy someone a beer.

Here I was, at a nightclub in Peru, and I'd suddenly gone from being alone to drinking at a Halloween party, backstage, with a DJ and his friends. All I'd had to do was say yes. I walked out of my hostel unsure and my night turned into an adventure when I stopped holding back.

Every once in a while someone would order shots and, like a game, a few would spill and the accused would be forced to order a new round. They came in waves of tequila, and rum, and sometimes Pisco, and we all became louder and more animated. The music got louder as the club got more raucous. The crowd pressed towards the DJ booth below us, dancing hard and tight. From my vantage point I felt each of my five senses become excited. It was unreal. In that moment, I was happy.

Later, I went with my "Fiesta Amigo" (as I had by that time named him) to get some Pisco Sours at the bar. I'd suggested it after I'd told him about my previous experience with the local drink. We were of course shouting at each other, but he spoke a little English. His name was Sebastien and he worked for an advertising agency downtown and he'd learned English when he went to university in Miami.

As we waited for our drinks, I pulled out my cellphone. With one eye closed I tried to focus on the time: 2:30.

"*Salud*," we said, like we had done many times already, and clinked our glasses together. When we got back to our table behind the DJ booth, I sat down across from Sebastien's girlfriend. She leaned into the table and I felt her tap my leg with her knuckles.

Looking down, I saw her hand clenched in a fist on top of my knee. I slid my open hand under hers to accept whatever she was handing me. I opened it towards me to see what it was—there was a small plastic bag with white powder and a key inside.

Well I wasn't expecting that to happen, I thought, but given where I was it didn't surprise me that much either. It's not like this is my first time behind a DJ booth at a party like this, and I am in South America—weirder things have happened.

In most situations I'd pass. I'm old enough to have seen drugs ruin friends' lives, and I've gone through my experimental phase in my early twenties. At least, that's how I feel about cocaine when I'm sober. In my drunken state, though, my mind only had two brilliant words: "Fuck it!"

Fuck it! I'm in Peru, and *Fuck it!* this stuff is probably more pure than anything I've tried before, and *Fuck it!* it's Halloween.

This is part of the reason I'm traveling to begin with, isn't it? I wanted to experience new customs and traditions. In the name of cultural research, I'll say yes to everything.

"When in Rome!" I said aloud to no one but myself and fumbled with the key as I tried to take a bump, or *punito* as Sebastien called it, that was smallish yet still sizable enough to be effective. I passed it back to his girlfriend under the table and, in a much more experienced way, they each took two *punitos* as methodically as taking a shot. We resumed scream-talking back and forth over the loud music with Sebastien translating as best he could.

As the soft edges of my drunken haze sharpened, the conversation went past where I could keep up, and I decided it was time to say *adios* to my new friends and enter the dance floor. We all hugged goodbye and I hopped past the DJ into the sea of people.

I caught a glimpse of myself in a mirror behind one of the bars. The reason I could see myself is because I stood out so awkwardly. I stood about a foot taller and about eight shades whiter than everyone surrounding me, and I was the only one who looked like a skateboarder. After trying to dance with some local girls (I am equally untalented at dancing and speaking Spanish), I awkwardly withdrew to the bar. After I ordered a final Pisco Sour, I sat down to think about what to do next.

It was pretty late, I was pretty drunk, and I knew I should quit while I was ahead and walk back to my hostel. I sold myself on the idea and walked back out the doors I'd come through.

Once on the street, I saw that most people had retreated to the safety of their homes and bedrooms by this time at night, the streets hollow and empty. I knew only the truly gluttonous were pursuing their wayward desires at this time of night.

A couple blocks from my hostel, the street got darker in a place where two of the street lights were shattered above. Right when I was in the middle of the darkest part I heard a quick, sharp whistle from under a small archway. *I know that whistle*, I thought. It was the whistle I'd heard the first night I was here, the night I got lost.

I scanned the streets to see if there was anybody else watching us and then turned my attention towards whoever the midnight caller might be.

"Coca," he said, stepping toward me.

I walked underneath the shadowy doorway. At this point I didn't want to fuck around with Spanish translations and I asked in English, "How much?"

"Tween-tee Soles," he said, looking around while I did the currency conversion in my head. Twenty Peruvian Soles was approximately $8USD.

"Ok," I said.

He reaches his hand out with an open palm.

"You give me 20 Soles, I buy."

"You don't have?" I asked.

"*No, yo vamos*," he said motioning down the street with his arm. "My name is Michael, *soy honesto*." He tapped his heart twice, repeating, "*Mi amigo, yo soy honesto*."

Fuck it. I turned my shoulder so he couldn't see how much money I had in my wallet and I handed him a 20 Sole bill. He shoved it in his pocket and spit out a few Spanish sentences, from which I only understood "*honesto*" and "*cinco minutos*." *I guess I'll wait for him here*, I thought.

To be honest, by the time Michael turned the corner at the end of the street, I couldn't have cared less whether he came back. The small *punito* I'd taken in the club had worn off long before, and I was so drunk that going to bed seemed like more attractive than conducting any more "cultural research" at this time of night. On the other hand, I already paid the man, and the devil inside wanted to play, so there wasn't much I could do but sit and wait for Michael to return.

After 10 or 15 minutes, I realized my "*honesto*" friend had ripped me off. But instead of repeating my mantra of *fuck it*, my mind began repeating, *fuck that guy*. I'd been duped by a piece of shit street bum!

I flicked my half-finished cigarette into the street and shouted "Fuck that guy!" Jumping up from the curb, I drunkly marched back to the hostel. I'm just angry I let a bum rip me off. All day, I've been trying to decide what I am going to do if I cross paths with Michael again.

My conclusion is quite simple—I'm going to smash his toes with my skateboard.

I don't want to cause a big scene in the street. I'm just going to walk up, slam the tail of my board onto his toes, then walk away. I don't want "*Honesto* Michael" to forget who I am, and having to rip off tourists with a sore foot will be a certain reminder.

I'm angrier at myself than at Michael. I was the one who gave my money away and watched it run off down the street. Still, *fuck that guy*.

Chapter Four
WHEREVER I MAY ROAM (IN THE STREETS OF MIRAFLORES)

FRIDAY, NOVEMBER 2
4:30pm, Angel Hostel

Just like a typical tourist, I ate at Burger King today and used their Wi-Fi. I called my sister Emily on Skype and she helped me find a new perspective, which was good. I was feeling pretty down.

The last couple days, my mind has been filled with all kinds of questions, and I've felt pretty lonely. Getting lonely while traveling alone is normal, but I've also been thinking about my past, and why I've suffered during so much of it. What the hell is the point of it all, of all the pain one must go through in life?

After speaking with Emily, I saw things differently and that refreshed my attitude in a much-needed way. It made me feel more positive about the choice I made to come here and travel alone. She's traveled to Asia, India, and a bunch of other places, so I trust her advice.

Sometimes my thoughts run away from me, and I like to hear the opinion of somebody I trust: it helps me hold on to what's real. Emily's simple and clear encouragement untangled some of my emotions. In the end, she made everything seem less complicated.

I'm fortunate to have the family I do. They try their best to understand me, even though I don't think they have the slightest idea about all the problems I've had.

It'd be nice to believe humans were meant to live a better life, a happy life. Don't we all ask ourselves these kinds of questions? Don't we all want to reach some kind of conclusion as to what it all means?

The problem is I'm just not as talented at ignoring these questions as other people are.

Skateboarding has helped me figure out how to get around Miraflores, but I still feel lost. Going around the city, I feel like I'm inside of myself. Not only am I one of the few Westerners here, I'm one of the worst Spanish speakers as well, and the way people stare at me when I try to speak to them I might as well be an alien. Even though I'm surrounded by humans, I feel more alone than if I was stranded on a deserted island.

The biggest challenge I will face on this trip is going to be overcoming my personal issues. Before I came, I just assumed the traveling part would be the most difficult, but it's not. I think that what I'm going through now will be the most challenging: coming into contact with parts of myself that I mask or tuck away when I'm at home.

When I'm at home, surrounded by people I know, and this holds true for most of us, I play my part in a role I've created for myself. I fulfill my social obligations, and conform to the rules of society, acting in what I've determined is an acceptable way. Don't we all do this? Deciding each day when we look in the mirror whether or not to continue acting out our role we've created?

This is why it is paramount to travel alone. When you travel alone, you're instantly set free from this character you've assumed. When you travel alone, no one knows who you are, there's no predetermined idea about how you should act, you are free, and you can be your true self. Every morning you are liberated to create your identity as you truly want it to be.

I'll always be a male who grew up in Canada, and that's part of my character, but the essence, the truth that my character is built from, is formed anew continuously. I generate myself in each moment by my actions and decisions. When I travel alone, I'm free to be myself, in a way that I can only describe as being pure and natural.

At the core of who I am, I'd like to think I'm a good person, a happy person, a kind person. Yet for me to reach these virtuous layers, first I have to shed the layers of vice that I've piled on top. Lima isn't the easiest place to be vulnerable, which is why vices are helpful. They give me something to hold on to when real life feels slippery.

The city and the cultural barrier make me feel isolated, and I'll be even more isolated next week when I'm in the jungle, where I will undoubtedly examine myself more closely. I'll be able to let down my defenses, and I hope to dig below my layers of vice, uncovering the virtuous parts I know are part of who I am.

Besides calling Emily, I haven't spoken much in the last few days. There hasn't been much need to, not after seeing what little I can accomplish with Spanish. I've had one conversation going on constantly, and it's in English, too. The only problem is that it's been with myself, in my mind.

One week ago, I was in San Francisco and I saw more people than I'd ever seen talking to themselves in the streets. They were the kind of people you'd think of if I asked you to think of a "crazy homeless person." Did you picture a white-haired guy wearing bathroom slippers, a dress suit, and talking out loud about an obscure conspiracy theory? He was there.

Most *sane* people would say someone who talks to themselves has gone *insane,* but as I roam the streets of Miraflores there's a stream of conversation inside my mind. I think my thoughts are in English, but perhaps they're just English names given to the forms of what I'm thinking about, or perhaps they become English when I vocalize them? Sometimes I think the only difference between the crazy people in San Francisco and me is that they were vocalizing their personal conversations while I, the *sane* one, instead has conversations in my mind. What's the difference between us? Am I a mute lunatic? And if so, aren't we all?

I'm happy and totally exhausted from skating so much. My brain is tired from assimilating so much new, unique stimuli. Paying for a private room was a great decision: it's like having my own little Canadian embassy. If things get too crazy out in the city, I can always retreat back here.

I'll rest for another half-hour and then walk up to Kennedy Park to get some dinner. The sun goes down at 6pm so it's the perfect time to watch the sideways rays get cast across the city.

Now that I think about it, the hell with walking, I'm going to skate. Maybe I'll meet some fellow travelers or skater friends along the way—and if I'm lucky, I'll run into Michael and get the chance to smash his goddamn toes.

Chapter Five
LIFT OFF

SATURDAY, NOVEMBER 3
11:47am, Star Peru flight 3115, seat 14A

Hiding behind dark sunglasses, I'm trying to escape the daylight coming through the tiny airplane window. I feel like absolute dog shit. My head is pounding as we lift off from Lima on our way into the Amazon. My view of the shacks and shanty villages surrounding the airport becomes smothered by thick gray clouds. When we reach our cruising altitude, the vibration of the plane soothes me into a relaxed state.

I'm leaning my head against the double-paned window and replaying events from last night in my mind. The sound of my voice is drowned out by blaring prop-plane engines when I mutter, "Never again! I'm here to figure my shit out. No more partying!" I laugh and my shoulders bounce against the back of my seat—*what an insane night.*

I'd just finished eating amazing ceviche at a seafood restaurant near

Kennedy Park. The sun had set, but it was early dusk and still light. I had my headphones on, skating back to my hostel and listening to Edward Sharpe and the Magnetic Zeros.

I ollied up a curb, swung wide around a fire hydrant, and turned down the street to my hostel. Then all of a sudden—Boom!—I ran right into that lousy bum Michael. He stood in front of me, and I felt my brain click when I realized who it was. I picked up my board and stood over him.

I became aware that I was so much bigger than him, I could have put him on the ground in many different ways. My blood was pumping, and there were drops of sweat sliding down my temples. All the anger I had felt came rushing back to into me. I wasn't scared, but I could see he was. It was a difficult emotion to suppress. My shoulder muscles began to coil, and my arm cocked back, ready to swing.

"*Lo siento, lo siento,*" he sputtered, his mouth starting to quiver, remembering who I was.

Before I could say anything, he'd reached into his pocket and pushed his hand into mine. I took a half-step backwards. *What the fuck just happened?* I thought, trying to determine if I should stay, swing at him, or skate away.

"*Lo siento, no gustaria problemas mi amigo, por favor.*" Michael repeated some shit about how sorry he was.

While he stood in front of me submissively, I decided to throw my board down under my feet and put my left hand on his shoulder. Looking him directly in the eyes, I knew there was no need for violence.

"*No problema,* Michael," I said, to which he bowed his head, and again repeated how sorry and honest he was. But I just wanted closure from everything to do with him. I rode off, saying, "*Hasta luego, amigo.*"

I waited until a few blocks later before inconspicuously reaching into my pocket to check out what he'd given me. It had all happened so fast. It was a little plastic bag. I stood under a tree and looked at it. I squeezed it between my thumb and finger, and then opened a corner of it to hold it up to my nose. It had a sharp and bitter smell. There was no mistake: it was cocaine, and more than I knew what the hell to do with.

When I lived in Canada, I think the price was $80 a gram. But that's nothing compared to what some Aussie friends told me. They said it went for $300 a gram, and it was shit quality where they live.

I'd given Michael the equivalent of eight American dollars and he'd run off with it, but just now in his terror, he'd handed me four, maybe five, grams of Peruvian cocaine. He went from the bum that ripped me off to the guy that was sorry for being late on his delivery. It was an interesting lesson in global economics.

Skating back to my hostel, I got excited for some *real* cultural experience. It was, if I could believe him, "*purifico cocaine.*" With the abundance of cocaine in South America, and because it's so cheap to make, I guessed this stuff was as pure as it got. I won't pretend I'm an expert, but I've done enough research on this place to know to a few things about it.

Canada has weed, France has wine, Peru has cocaine. In the name of cultural research, I said *Fuck It.* This wasn't a Christian summer camp. I did come on this trip to better myself, but I also came to have new experiences.

When I got back to the hostel, I casually greeted Jose and locked myself in my room. I plugged my phone into my portable speaker and put on The Rolling Stones' "Sweet Virginia."

The baggie Michael had given me had a smiley-face sticker on it which must have been the branding for whoever he got it from. I went over to The Mothership (the bag I carry on planes with me) to pull out the *Psychology Today* I'd bought on my layover in Houston, and I sat down on the bed and poured a little of the flaky white powder onto the back cover.

I got up and grabbed my plane ticket from on top of the TV and pulled a card out of my wallet. I ripped off the ticket stub and rolled it into a tube, then sat back down and chopped two small lines.

I lifted the magazine up to my face with my left hand. With my right hand, I held the rolled up plane ticket inside my nostril using the pressure of my thumb to hold the other nostril closed.

Intake one...........Bing!

Intake two..............Bang!

I walked out of my room, across the kitchen, and into the bathroom. I checked my nose in the mirror to see if there was anything visible, but there wasn't, so I went back to my room and sat on the bed.

I didn't feel anything. I wondered *did I do enough?* Like I said, I wouldn't consider myself an expert. *Come on!*, I thought, *this is Peru, what's all the hype about?* Sitting there, still not feeling anything, I picked up the rolled-up ticket stub and chopped two more lines, slightly bigger this time.

Intake one.................... Bing!

Intake two......................Bang!

I checked my nose in the bathroom mirror again. When I pushed it around with my finger I realized something—the reason I hadn't felt anything when I'd been sitting on my bed was because my whole face was fucking numb!

I laughed and thought about a scene in the movie *Blow*, when Johnny Depp brings a new supply of cocaine to be tested by a specialist. While the guy is measuring its purity by testing its melting point, he tries a line and with a surprised look he shouts, "I can't feel my face. I mean, I can touch it, but I can't feel it inside!"

A tinge of guilt rippled through me. I hurried back to my room and sat down on the bed next to my *Psychology Today* magazine. I tried to quickly make amends with myself for what I'd just done. It took determination, but I overruled the thought *What the fuck am I doing?* with the fail-safe *Fuck it!*

Fuck it, I thought, *I'll need to get serious about the reason I'm here soon enough, but I might as well get this out of my system now. I've sinned plenty worse in my life, and while this isn't a personal high point, I've hit much lower, and this is my last night in Lima.*

Miraflores was not just my base camp, it had become my devil's lair. I'll start my special diet tomorrow, this is my final chance for one last party.

Everything in moderation, right? Even moderation?

Those lines got me all pumped up, and when I came back to my room, I listened to music and worked on my writing. At some point

I decided to go out and find a party, but before I left I slid the magazine towards me one more time. Bing! Bang!

The street where I'd been on Halloween was packed with people. I wandered in and out of different bars, with different music, and worked towards quenching an enormous thirst, but I felt like an outsider in all of them.

I tried to start random conversations, but my inability to understand Spanish made it next to impossible. Most people just stared at me, then through me, and then they dismissed me. I gave up trying.

Later in the night, I found a club with good music but I don't remember much after that. It's all mixed into one drunk, high, foggy, deep-house infused, memory.

I went home sometime around 3 AM and didn't have any problems this time. There was of course a huge bag of coke in my room, though, and there was no way I was going to bring it with me to the airport today.

Jose was the only person I could think to give it to, but I couldn't give drugs to a young kid. After conducting a little more cultural research in my room, for Peru's sake, I got an idea, and taped the bag underneath the bed frame. So, at some point in the future of the Angel Hostel in Lima, Peru, room number 6, someone's going to find two stickers under the head of the bed with the cover of a psychology magazine folded up, and a little plastic bag with a smiley face and a few grams of pure Peruvian cocaine inside.

I feel like the absolute definition of a hungover person. I didn't puke last night, but that's just a testament to my current tolerance to alcohol. I don't have enough fingers on my hands to count the number of Pisco Sours I drank, and at any point just thinking about them might make me puke.

I'm sitting on this small plane after the longest two hour wait at the airport and I can honestly say I'm done partying. I truly need the natural way of life I came here to find, but in my immediate future I just need a bed.

I have no idea what to expect when I arrive in Iquitos, but I need to figure out how I'm going to get from there to the shaman's house in the jungle.

Looking out the oval, slightly frosty window, I see the never-ending Amazon rainforest and I feel more peaceful the further we fly into it. When I walked out of the airport, I felt more self-confident than I had when I was outside the airport in Lima. As a traveler I was starting to feel steadier in my steps. Maybe I was just in an ignorant state at the time (which happens when you're hungover), or maybe I truly was more stable. Either way, I wasn't stressed out and it felt like I was standing on the offensive, instead of the defensive as I had been before.

I was glad I decided to spend a couple days in Lima to help me adjust to South America. I felt a bit more prepared for whatever might happen, besides, life is unexpected and that's the only thing I *should* expect!

Inside the airport I said goodbye to the kind, yet somewhat detestable, tourists I'd sat next to on the plane. They were a group of 20-something-year-old Asian-Americans that went to Arizona State University. They came together to South America for a self-proclaimed *extreme adventure*. I guess it's kind of what I am trying to do, but with a very different agenda.

They'd changed planes in Lima after coming from Cuzco where they had hiked the Inca trail. Kelvin, the leader of the group I'd sat next to, told stories about the guides that led them to Machu Picchu.

They made their *extreme adventure,* if you can call it that, sound pretty disgusting. In essence, they'd paid to be shepherded up a path, with guides and donkeys doing all the hard work. They didn't even set up their own tents or need to carry anything more than a small pack each day.

I'm looking for the opposite kind of adventure. I'm happy to do my own work. I know I'll only get the real rewards I want from overcoming real challenges.

Waiting for my bags, I couldn't help chuckling when I looked at them standing together in their perfectly planned outfits. They were wearing brands like REI, North Face, and Patagonia, and they looked like they'd just stepped out of the pages of a mountain-sportswear catalogue.

They all were wore semi-new hiking boots(five days in Cuzco, plus the day back home that they'd all hiked some hill near their campus), they wore loose-fitting, khaki-style cargo pants, and to top it off they all had different variations of the same multi-pocketed, long-sleeve shirts. They were the kind of outfits which probably cost more than the average year's salary for a person living in Iquitos.

I was wearing shorts, skate shoes, and a dirty t-shirt that had small spots of blood from when I fell skateboarding down the sidewalk with Big Red and The Mothership strapped to me. There was a big bruise on my shin from when I was at the skatepark the other day, and my hands were stained with ink from writing (which is the fun/ridiculous part of using a fountain pen made in the 80's).

Right after we had taken off, Kelvin showed me the manicure he got the day before in Cuzco. He explained it was normal for men in Peru to get manicures and I nodded my head like I understood what the hell he was talking about. He said it's obvious to see which men have to work hard labor for their jobs, and a manicure shows you're not part of the shameful "working class." He looked shocked when I showed him my hands.

I told him, "I'm proud to work with my hands." Through my eyes, when I looked over my scars, I saw stories.

From what he'd told me on the plane, it sounded like where they were heading now was quite a lavish jungle retreat. The kind of place where you could see toucans at breakfast, and swim in an infinity pool at lunch, and sleep in rooms with A/C, and enjoy all those other fancy Western necessities we think we need to enjoy ourselves.

This was validated when I watched their big bags roll onto the conveyor belt and they pointed them out one by one to porters that had already been assigned to help the group, who worked furiously to stack the bags on as few carts as possible.

The group followed a man out of the airport who was wearing a collared golf-shirt that had a logo on the breast pocket, and the porters were behind them. They crossed the parking lot, the porters wheeling the carts with all the bags that had never once been touched by the group.

They were all herded, with another couple that was on the plane with us, towards a private bus. The couple followed the leader up the stairs, and the ASU group stopped beside the bus to take a group selfie (shot by a manicured photographer).

Behind them on the side of the bus an inspirational quote was written in flowing handwriting—*Find your Spirit*—I wondered if they thought it was that easy.

It was all I needed to see to confirm I'd made the right choice to do this trip as a solo backpacker. I'm damn happy I'm not stuck following a herd of Americans and taking a bus to *find my spirit*. If I ever make an online reservation to *find my spirit*, shoot me. I feel bad for them, really. They are young and impressionable; they'll probably believe anything they're told once they get out there.

I fell for that trick once, but not anymore. I'll make my own choices about what I believe from here on out. Back when I was young(er) and (more) foolish I decided to get involved with the church and religion. It all started naturally enough. They were the only place in my small town that had skateboard ramps.

The people were all nice enough, and there was even the chance to hang out with girls, which alongside skateboarding, were the bane of my existence at the time. I believed these men and women who told me what was important to believe. For the most part, these lessons did me no harm.

There was no anger or malice in their lessons, but I never met anyone who didn't in some way contradict their own principles. They tried to tell me there was only one way—their way—of finding my spirit, God's spirit, and ultimately, the almighty Holy Spirit.

It's one thing for a man to go into the world and try to place his moral sensibilities within the context of an outdated story like the Bible. But it's a completely different thing to preach its nonsensical wisdom and then leave the church in your Mercedes. As Nietzsche said, "Faith: not wanting to know what is true."

I want to know what is true, so instead of putting my faith in another man's idea of what's true, I'll search for truth inside of me. I'm in Peru for my own kind of adventure. I have my own questions I want answers to, and that means having courage, it means breaking free from the custom-tailored tourist experience, and most importantly it means I've got to do this on my own. Besides, I couldn't afford their luxury retreat anyway.

I needed to get a taxi into the city of Iquitos, find a hotel, and hopefully in the next day or two I figure out how to get to the shaman's property.

My friend Kari gave me loose directions:

Get off at KM50 and take the trail on the left hand side of the road. You will follow this for two miles before you get to her house. It will cross over a little bridge near the beginning at some point. I told her you were coming but didn't know your exact date so she's expecting you sometime this month. Watch out for snakes! Just kiddin, have fun :).

The problem is, her message seemed too cryptic for me to be comfortable enough to hike alone into the jungle on my first day. I had to find someone in town who knew how to get there.

Dismissing the first few taxi drivers that approached me, I locked eyes with a driver with a funny smile who was too small to overpower me. He walked up to me and took Big Red, something I now know to expect. I followed him from under the shade of the airport's faded-blue awning into the bright Amazonian heat.

The pack I had on my back, The Mothership, is a gray-and-black backpack made by Nixon and I carry it with me at all times. Everything inside is important and I am keenly aware I must never lose it or let it get stolen. It wouldn't be the end of the world, but it would make the world more difficult.

Inside is my computer, a leather-bound journal my sister Jillian gave me, three paperback books (*Why I am so Wise* by Friedrich Nietzsche, *Existentialism is a Humanism* by Jean-Paul Sartre, and *The Apology* by Plato).

I have headphones, an iPhone charger, two USB flash drives, a deck of playing cards, sunglasses, a sleeping mask, a harmonica in the C-chord, a miniature Native American dream catcher, a 1980s Schaffer Delta grip fountain pen, two cheaper uni-ball pens, a 3.5 mm headphone cord (so I can connect my iPhone to any stereos I come across), my Canadian passport, and my American work visa (so I can get through customs back in the States when I go home).

The Mothership has two straps on the back that holds my skateboard and on the top strap I have the Thai prayer flag Kelsey gave to me tied in a knot. I like it because it's authentic. She got it for me last year when she got back from a family vacation in Thailand.

Getting a gift someone got for you when they were traveling is special, and I've had it tied to my bag ever since. It's gone all over the world with me; it reminds me of her and it feels lucky. At first I thought the dragon-face design was creepy, but she told me that it's part of their culture and the dragon-face is meant to look scary in order to ward off bad spirits. So far, no encounters with bad spirits.

Ahead of me was my taxi driver and I watched Big Red bob up and down on his back as we walked across the parking lot.

It's a classic North Face 65L hiking backpack, and inside, I packed every item I thought I'd need on a five week jungle adventure. In the main compartment I packed an extra pair of shoes, a pair of hiking boots, a towel, 12 T-shirts, two pairs of jeans, two pairs of shorts, two pairs of boardshorts, one sweatshirt, a rain jacket, eight pairs of socks, seven pairs of boxers, and one nice dress shirt (in case I have any formal invitations).

And of course, in the middle of it all I included my trusty wizard cap. It was given to me at the Coachella music festival last spring, and you never know when you might need a wizard cap.

I rolled these items up tightly (rolling takes up less space than folding), and included a toiletry bag with all the regular manly supplies, a bottle of heavy-duty DEET bug spray, and a small first aid kit (one that I made, not the crappy pre-packed ones you get at the supermarket). In the inner pockets I brought my portable Nixon speaker, some random skateboard parts, and a couple gifts that I brought with me for the shaman.

I scanned the small parking lot and noticed, besides the chartered bus closing its doors, there were only a few *actual* cars. I grinned when it dawned on me that we were walking towards a small pack of three-wheeled motorcycle-taxi hybrids parked under the shade of a tall tree.

"*Esta es mi Motokar,*" my driver said as he pointed to a blue-flamed machine. There was a decal, *RTM-150G,* on the front fender of a modified motorcycle, and in the back were two wheels underneath a frame. It had a bench seat for passengers and a roof with tassels hanging from it. The whole thing was pretty rickety, but I could tell he'd put some effort into making it unique, and I liked that.

I sat behind hiems with my bags stacked next to me. We drove out of the airport and over the last speed-bump. He clicked through the gears and we chunkily picked up speed. The small engine rattled and vibrated, and every time he twisted the throttle it shook my seat.

I gulped down a huge breath of moist jungle air. I could taste the freshness of the oxygen that poured from the jungle. Once we'd reached our cruising speed I let the natural breeze wash the last bits of Lima away from me. The scent of the jungle air, the viscosity, it's so...Alive!

"Como se llama?" I recited after looking up from the Spanish phrase book app on my iPhone.

"Luis," he said, turning his head around and smiling at me.

"Yo nombre is Sean."

"Mucho gusto John!" he said as he took his left hand off the handlebar and raised it in a fist over his shoulder to give me an upside down fist bump.

"A donde vas?" he asked.

"No comprende," I said, cause yeah, I had no idea what he was saying.

"Donde esta su hotel?" he rephrased the question. *Ahhh*, I thought, *hotel, I know that word...*

However, unlike when I landed in Lima, I didn't have a reservation anywhere. I've learned when you're off the beaten path, sometimes the best places to stay get popular from word of mouth. Some don't even need websites. In those cases, it is only the rich, gringo-operated businesses that have websites, and they cater to a different type of tourist.

I decided I was going to try to use my good judgment and find a place to stay near the plaza in the center of town. *"Plaza de Armas,"* I leaned forward and told Luis. I typed a sentence into the phrase-book on my phone. *"Yo no hotel, Centro por favor."*

The *Plaza de Armas* is surrounded by hotels and restaurants and close by, next to the river, is the *Belén Market*. It's one of the largest outdoor markets in the Amazon, and a trading hub for over 150 small villages. Iquitos itself is the fifth-largest city in Peru, and the largest city in the Peruvian rainforest. I also read it's the largest city in the world not accessible by road—to get here you either have to take a boat or a plane.

It's as big as it is because there was a big influx of industry during the rubber boom of the 1900s. It brought a lot of social and economic influence from Europe—which came to an abrupt halt once the British cloned the rubber tree seeds and began growing them independently.

The road we drove on through the outskirts of town was a dirty blond color. The clouds of dust along it had, over time, painted the walls of the small shops and homes that faced the street. There were small groups of houses with shoeless children running back and forth between them.

We passed a gated army school with packs of boys in front. They were marching across the field and I could just hear their chanting voices over the two-stroke engine in our Motokar. Those sights soon dissolved and we crossed the threshold into the city. The traffic got denser, more cars mixed in with all the Motokars now. It was not a fancy metropolis, but it was definitely a city.

It seemed like the rules of driving in Iquitos had more in common with video games than real world driving. It reminded me of playing life-sized games of Mario Kart at Ryan Sheckler's house (the first professional skateboarder I coached to an X-Games Gold medal). He had a 15-foot TV installed in his game room and from behind my little Peruvian driver, my vantage point looked quite similar.

Each driver fought their way through traffic and tried to pass as many other Motokars as they could. Like a game of chess, they planned each pass two moves ahead. My driver Luis, was a master—as a driving and racing enthusiast, I appreciated how he strategically made each pass.

It didn't stop. Every time the light went green, off we'd go. To the left of the big bus, outside the right lane to pass a slower group of Motokars, between two vans, into the opposite lane, charging to the front of the pack at a red light, and then when the light went green, cutting everyone off racing towards the next pack of competitors to overtake.

It probably sounds more dangerous than it was. But to be honest, it was hard not to laugh at their initial speed, or lack thereof. When the light would change they'd crank their throttles, but nobody's Motokar could go faster than 50 km/h, and on the tiny 150cc engines it took about 30 seconds and four gears to get there.

For such an unknown city, Iquitos is gigantic! We passed street after street filled with people as far as I could see. It was a little grungy, but was also filled with tons of life, and it felt like a *real* city. When I say that, I mean New York, not Los Angeles, or in Canada I'd say Vancouver, not Calgary.

Small men with deep-creased wrinkles and golden skin on the back of their necks pushed beer-carts from corner to corner. There were stands with colorful umbrellas and baskets full of fruit that hung down, and next to them were the old ladies selling the fruit and sitting on upside down buckets. Along the telephone wires that crossed each intersection, there were banners tied up announcing local events and political candidates, both past and yet to come.

Luis dropped me off on the Southwest corner of the *Plaza de Armas*. I knew it was that corner because of the angle of the sun.

I waited until the next pack of Motokars had passed me before I crossed the street. With minimal effort, I let my skateboard, and gravity, assist me down the hill and towards a sign for the *Hotel La Casona*.

A half a block later, I angled across the street and jumped off my board onto the curb. When I bent down to grab my board, a small stream of sweat dripped off my pinky finger. And when I opened the door to the hotel, the arctic blast from the air-conditioning felt like it was trying to push me back outside. But I fought back. I wanted in.

It *whoosh*ed shut on a spring behind me, and as I waited for the receptionist, I wiped my forehead with my shirtsleeve. I was exhausted, hungover, sweaty, hungry, and that air-conditioning saved my life.

Before anyone had come to greet me, I'd already made the decision to stay. I didn't want to go back outside no matter what it cost—but luckily I was in a small jungle city in the Amazon, and a couple nights here was even cheaper than Lima.

WELCOME TO THE JUNGLE

CHAPTER SIX
STARTING FRESH

SUNDAY, NOVEMBER 4
1:45pm, The embankment above the river in Iquitos

After I got my hotel room yesterday, I took a shower and changed into non sweat-soaked clothes. I searched online and found a couple restaurants that served food that is ok to eat from when on the *Ayahuasca diet.* All I know is that I can't eat most of the stuff I usually do:
milk
cheese
yogurt
sour cream
fermented foods
meat or meat products
salt
sugary or sweet foods, including honey
chocolate
caffeine
hot or spicy foods
fried fats or oils
alcohol
AND, for some reason, I have to abstain from all sexual activity. I

should have started this diet days ago, but better late than never, right?!

I left the hotel and walked up the street to the Plaza de Armas. I was heading to a restaurant called The Yellow Rose of Texas, which I had seen when I got dropped off. I slid into a table underneath the shade from a faded red umbrella. The owner, a big oaf of a Texan, came out to greet me. Or came out to keep an eye on me, I'm not sure, but I didn't like his imposing vibe.

The sweat ran down his brow even faster than my own, and he made racist jokes, and when I told him where I was from, he asked how "Hong-couver" was this time of year. When he walked away, I felt awkward. His racist monologue had included rants about the locals that worked for him as well as Peruvians in general. His tongue was loose enough it inspired me to ask him some direct questions when he came back out, but he never came back. The fat American pig, extorting tourists and demonizing his local employees, left quite a first impression. I'll never forget his last words about the Dodge Viper parked in his garage back home in Texas. Fuck that guy.

Soon after he walked away, a cute, kind, and intelligent waitress, who was clearly a local, came out to take my order. I pointed to the chicken breast sandwich and Acai smoothie from the Ayahuasca section of the menu. She nodded with a kind smile and then disappeared into the restaurant. Most of the restaurants in town were the bottom floor of small buildings with small hand-painted signs and names like *El Pescador*. Outside, on the cracked sidewalks, they all put plastic chairs and plastic tables for their patrons. I could tell how authentic the restaurants were by the number of locals eating there.

While I was sipping on my smoothie and waiting for my sandwich, a group of travelers sat down at the table next to me. They had Henna-painted hands, dirty clothes, and to my tired brain's delight, they all spoke English.

I listened to them talk about food like it was the first time they'd eaten in weeks. Some of them talked about extending their trip, some talked about leaving the next day, and they all talked about ice cream.

I introduced myself to Andy, the Englishman sitting next to me, and asked him where they'd come from. He told me they were getting back from a 10-day retreat at the "Maripoza Center". They'd spent the first few days detoxifying and cleansing, mainly to get comfortable being in the jungle. The second half of their retreat was focused around four Ayahuasca ceremonies.

From his description, it seemed pretty legit. It wasn't the kind of retreat the "uber-tourists" whom I'd met on the plane were going to. It was nice to hear about their experiences, and their description of the Ayahuasca ceremonies excited me.

Andy told me he liked the jungle so much he was going to rent an apartment in Iquitos for at least another month. With his big head of flowing golden hair pulled back behind a sweat-stained headband, he resembled Aslan from *The Chronicles of Narnia*. He told me he runs a website called Daygame.com. When I checked it out it turns out to be a website that exposes the finer points on how to pick up girls during the day.

I guess that's the benefit of owning a website; as long as it makes money, you can work anywhere in the world with an Internet connection. The site surprised me, but who am I to pass judgment on a professional playboy that has a spiritual side. I chatted with some of the others. The whole group was buzzing. Maybe it was the ice cream, or maybe it was because they just finished their retreat, but they all seemed pretty charged up.

—I love how this humid weather makes the pages of my notebook soft like cloth. It swallows the ink from my pen in a way I've never experienced. In Canada, the cold makes the paper more stiff and feel crispier. The heat here might make my writing look more messy, but it also fills it with emotion, and I like that.

—Shit, It's too hot to be writing outside, I'm going to go enjoy take advantage of having a room with A/C while I still have it.

2:30pm, Hotel La Casona.

Ahh, the refreshing arctic air in my air-conditioned room, I'll continue.

After I ate at the Yellow Rose, I told the group from the Maripoza Center I'd try to find them later and went back to my hotel so I could reply to some emails and escape the heat.

After sending off a few work emails, I got too restless to sit in my room and went outside to smoke a cigarette I watched the sun splash the last of its light through the city as it began to set.

I spotted Luis, the Motokar driver I'd met at the airport, on the curb across the street from my hotel. He was laughing with a couple of other drivers and smoking a cigarette. Their eyes were bloodshot from driving on the dusty streets all day. Luis threw his arms in the air when he saw me and shouted, "*Hola amigo!*" motioning for me to come over to his Motokar.

Taking a drag of my American Spirit, I nodded my head to him, then walked across the street so we could talk without shouting.

"*Como estas?*" I said.

"*Todo bien!*" he cocked his right hand back to give me a friendly high five, "*Y tu?*" We finished our handshake with a fist pound—a global phenomenon, I swear.

"*Bien, Bien,*" I said, trying to sound smooth and indifferent.

The thing is, if you travel enough and meet enough people from different walks of life, you begin to understand a more universal language. The question I was asking him wasn't going to be a problem. Not for either of us. We had said hello with our words but with our body language, our eyebrow lifts, and the casual head nods. We'd had a side conversation at the same time.

"*Donde es marijuana?*" I asked, pinching my fingers together, and holding them up to my mouth like I was smoking a joint, already knowing the answer.

"Ahhh, *usted quiere comprar marihuana?*" He imitated my motion.

"*Si?*" I said unsurely. I only understood one word, but it *was* the one that mattered.

"*Ok Senor, no problema. Vamos!*" He waved his arm in a circle that ended with him pointing at his blue-flamed bike. I followed him towards it and got in, feeling a tiny wave of adrenaline. Luis seemed trustworthy, but I knew that the trip I'd signed up for was less than legal.

He brought his foot down on the kick-starter and the bike revved to life. The fresh breeze when we drove off was a welcome treat. I smiled to myself as we rumbled down the main street. I loved these kinds of adventures and wanted to smoke a joint.

"*Cuánto quiere comprar?*" He turned his head to ask me.

I blankly stared into the back of his head, unsure of what he'd said. "*Cuantro dinero?*" he said quickly, distracted by the road race we were in the middle of. The Motokar driver next to us glared over at us through blacked-out sunglasses. Luis hit the engine's limiter at the top of second gear and with a clunk he clicked the bike into third. We were soon passing 25 km/h and the race was on.

I couldn't really hear what Luis was saying, let alone translate his Spanish, but rubbing his fingers together over his shoulder, I realized he was asking me how much weed I wanted to buy.

I didn't have any idea how much weed costs in the Amazon, but I didn't mind spending a little money to get some. The sun sliced through the buildings and as we bumped along I imagined how great it would be to be in my private, air-conditioned room with its big comfy bed, cable TV, an ice-cold Coca-Cola, and a big fat joint.

I pulled $60 Soles ($20USD) from my wallet and tapped Luis on the shoulder, hoping it was enough for at least a few joints. He looked back quickly and grabbed the money with his non-throttle hand. He had to concentrate though; we were now racing a tanned, mini-Terminator-looking driver next to us.

We got to the outskirts of town and made a wide bumpy turn down a side street, the Motokar bucking in all directions as we sloshed through deep puddles and potholes. A few blocks later, the houses were in states of disrepair and we stopped next to one of the broken-down buildings.

I could see, through the open wall, a family in the kitchen eating dinner. I was staring at them in wonder the same way they were staring at me. There was a single lightbulb hanging above the kitchen table. I turned away and Luis dismounted. He tapped the bench seat and said, "*un momento, tu aca,*" pointing for me to stay in my seat.

He stepped into the house, walked past the family eating dinner and through a small door behind them. When I looked back at the family, they were still staring at me. I looked away again.

To avoid their gaze, I lit up a cigarette, leaned against the back of the bench seat, and stared up at the pink clouds.

The colors were soft and dusk splashed a warm glow over the building. The way the light hit the broken boards, plastic panels and aluminum sheets they were made of made them look like a pastel painting. Sitting in the back of Luis' Motokar and watching my first day in the Amazon shift towards night, was a memory I'll never forget.

Luis returned and handed me a football sized package wrapped in newspaper. I put it under my shirt and reached my fist out to give him a pound before he jumped back on the bike. We took off, speeding down the street and made our way towards the center of town and the Hotel La Casona.

When I got back to my room I smoked a joint. Luis had given me a bag from a loaf of bread that was more than half filled.Again, I had more than I knew what to do with. I lay under the A/C on my bed and listened to music. It was nice to feel my body relax and my thoughts slow. The weed was what you'd expect from organic jungle bush-weed, not too strong, but perfect for easing anxiety and relieving stress.

A little while later, I decided I should go get something to eat. This time I went to the Karma Cafe which is on the opposite corner of the plaza from the Yellow Rose. I was hoping to run into the group I met at lunch who said they'd be around there that evening.

I entered the funky restaurant and sat down on an empty couch in the corner. It gave me a good vantage point of the bar, and I digested the crowd, a mix of tourists, expats, and locals. It had a welcoming atmosphere and English menu's with an *Ayahuasca diet* section. All things considered, I'm not supporting that damn Texan anymore.

The dreamy electronic music was lowered and a skinny, dreadlocked, Gandalf-the-Wizard-looking guy named Radolpho introduced himself. He had a bag on his shoulder bulging with the contorted shapes of random instruments. After he unpacked them he gave a short speech in Spanish, of which I understood nothing.

He began his show by turning an eight-foot rain-shaker on its end.

The sounds of the seeds trickling down the hollow pole created a natural ambiance in the bar. The flute he blew into was made of light colored wood, and its melody became interwoven with the rain-shaker's peaceful rhythm.

One of the locals I'd walked past outside who had tried to sell me some of his artwork came into the cafe and sat down next to me. He was wearing a backwards Miami Heat hat, and had DC Shoes, and I'm pretty sure was the only one from his group that could speak any English.

"Hello my friend," he said, reaching his hand out to give me a fist-bump.

"*Hola*," I said back to him.

"Where you from?" His smile was authentic and his face was framed by his dirty, toothy grin.

"Vancouver, Canada." I said proudly. I don't care about how rich or famous my bloodline is, the fact my home country is globally respected is the greatest blessing I could have been given.

"Oh! Canada, I love Canada people. My friend is Canada. He come here and love the jungle."

"Oh yeah? Where was he from?" I asked.

"I don't know," he smiled. "My name Oscar, what you name?"

"Sean, nice to meet you," I said, and reached my hand out to give him a formal handshake, "Where do you live?"

"I live Belen." He said with an equal amount of pride as I'd said Canada and pointed towards the shack-village below the city and right on the edge of (and sometimes in) the river.

"You buy me beer, John?"

"Yeah sure, what do you want, and it's Sean not John."

"Shon?" He said once and then turned his head and ordered beers for both of us from the waitress. The waitress came back and handed us two *Pilsen Grande's*.

"*Salud*!" I said when we banged the big bottles against each other. We both took large sips and listened to the live and acoustic jungle-jam. But it wasn't long before Oscar turned to ask me another question.

"You buy *marihuana*?"

"No, I don't need any," I laughed; *where was he a few hours ago?* "Thanks though, I just got some."

He looked disappointed. "You want cocaine, I make you nose happy." He said as casually as if he was asking me to buy him another beer. I laughed, but then saw he was serious. *Hmmm, should I say fuck it?* I thought. *What do you want, brain? It is Saturday night... One last hurrah, and then I'll straighten out my act.*

I thought all of this while I heard myself say, "No, I don't need any coke, thanks though." I wanted to change the subject, so I raised my bottle in front of me to remind him I just bought him a beer, and we cheers'd again.

I didn't have to say *fuck it* tonight. I'd had my fun in Lima and I shouldn't have even been drinking that beer but I was trying to be polite. All I could think about was how done with partying I was.

"You look my art?" Oscar said timidly.

He did deserve credit for his persistence. "Yeah sure, *si por favor.*" I leaned forward to look into the backpack he was opening on the ground between us. He pulled out some bracelets made from colorful thread and handed them to me. He continued to dig through his stuff until he found what he was looking for.

"For you," he said. In his hands, he held an intricately woven, black-hemp necklace with a purple crystal laced into the middle of it.

"For me?" I asked. I wasn't sure if he was giving me a gift or if this was part of a scheme.

"*Si, es regala para tu.*" He slipped into his native Spanish tongue, but I think I understood.

He placed it on my neck. "You pay later," he said, and there was the catch.

"How much?" I liked the crystal; the simplicity of it was appealing.

"It has many power, is teaching crystal, is teach you about you."

"How much is it?" I just wanted a price.

"$300 Soles."

"Haha, no way!" It was way too much, I wasn't rich and $300 soles is close to $100USD. No way I was going to pay that.

"$200 Soles," he said quickly.

"No, it's ok, another time." I took off the necklace and handed it back to him. His face became sunken and he looked dejected. I felt bad for not giving him any money, but I did buy him a beer. I didn't have tons of money myself. I think at that point I had $600USD in my account.

I wanted to make him happy again. Like I said earlier, if there's one way to make a new friend in a foreign country, it's to buy a local a beer. I flagged the waitress over and said, "*Dos mas, por favor.*"

"Pilsen?"

"*Si, and la quinta por favor.*" I may have just been ordering a few beers, but I felt like my Spanish was improving.

When she brought the bill and two large beers, I asked Oscar if he wanted to go to the plaza. I hadn't seen any of the Maripoza group and I wanted to check if they were there. Perhaps optimistic about getting more free beers if he stuck with me, he jumped up and said, "We go!"

When we got to the plaza I saw a group of Westerners with similar Henna-painted hands but didn't see any of the guys I'd eaten lunch with. As we walked towards this new group, Oscar got called over by some friends.

I kept walking toward the group Henna-painted hands until I was within earshot of their English banter. I said hello to two young guys and a girl that were watching a puppy play in front of them. They turned and greeted me with calm, graceful smiles—very zen.

Paris was from Kentucky, but moved here a year ago with her "partner." They bought a property a short boat ride down the river. They split up not too long ago and she had been back in the States for the last few months. She came back to take care of some legal stuff with her property and timed her return with the 10-day retreat at the Maripoza Center with some of her friends. She told me she was planning to stay in town for a few more days to try and find work.

Of the two guys, Pedro was shorter and younger and he didn't talk much. He grew up in Minnesota and came for the retreat. He wanted to stay longer but he wasn't sure how long. He found the puppy they were playing with while they had been wandering the streets. It was a cute little mutt, must not have been much more than a couple months old.

The taller and wiser looking guy was Nick, from Colorado. He has been backpacking around this part of the Amazon for three months. For being just 21 years old, he had a decent beard, and even though we were strangers there was something about him that felt familiar. I liked him right away.

While Paris was planning on staying in Iquitos, Nick and Pedro said they were going to stay on her property. They needed a couple more days in town to get their supplies. One of the people they were waiting to meet up with is a white Shaman. They were intent on finding the strongest, purest Ayahuasca made and I guess this guy sold it.

It sounded interesting, and I asked if they were scared to drink Ayahuasca alone, without the guidance of a shaman. Nick answered by telling me they were confident they could "hold their own space" without any problems.

Paris had eyes which were distant, and yet at the same time alluring, tempting in the way all bright lights in the distance are. Her hair was tangled and messy, retaining a natural beauty. I wondered what lay so far away in those eyes. Her skin was a dark olive color and I could tell she was a soft girl who had spent many days kissed by the sun.

They told me all kinds of far-fetched things about their Ayahuasca ceremonies. Hearing one was ok, but it was hard to get interested in the mystical parts of their stories because they just sounded like crazy hallucinations. Maybe I didn't "get it" yet.

They were easy to connect with, but Pedro had a bit of a nervous temperament and only seemed concerned with his puppy. I felt awkward all of a sudden, and said goodbye to the group after exchanging email addresses with Paris and Nick.

Leaving them with the puppy, I wandered into the crowd and took my time to walk around the perimeter of the plaza on the way back to my hotel.

I made another new friend, an older man standing outside my hotel and smoking a cigarette when I walked up. He looked East Indian, but said he was from Peru. He had lived in Iquitos for over

20 years and his name was Raul.

He spoke English really well, with an accent I couldn't place, and his voice was rough and gravelly, maybe the remnants of years of heavy drinking and smoking.

I told him I came to Iquitos to find my way to a Shaman's house, a Donna Otillia.

Raul's eyes lit up and he told me he had her number and could call her. While digging with one hand in his pocket for his cellphone, he asked me what I was going to do there. I told him I wanted to live on her land and study the plant medicines.

I couldn't believe my luck; I hadn't even begun to figure out how I was going to get there, and here was someone who could call her and talk to her in Spanish for me.

He reached into his pocket and pulled out an old scratched up cellphone. Scrolling through his contacts, he turned the backlit screen towards me. "Look, I have all the shamans numbers," he said and clicked on Donna Otillia's number then leaned back against the wall of the hotel when it began to ring.

Once she answered, Raul began a rapid conversation in Spanish with her. My friend Kari had previously sent an email to Otillia and told her I'd be coming so I was hoping she would know who I am.

"Sean from Canada," I told Raul, the easiest way I could think of explaining who I am. He spoke Spanish too quickly for me to understand anything, so I just stood there waiting for him to hang up and explain everything to me in English.

He lowered the phone from his ear and ended the call. Smiling at me, he told me he had made a plan for her to meet me outside my hotel on Monday morning at 11 AM.

It was the best way my night could have ended. Raul sorted out how I was going to get to the shamans. He stood there leaning against the wall, but before I went into the hotel, I gave him $10 soles. I winked and said *salud*, thankful for his help, but also saying cheers for the cold beer I imagined he was going to go buy.

I felt a rush of concern when I woke up this morning. I'm worried that my time with Otillia might not be a strong enough experience for me. I'm not sure if what I'm looking for is more than what she offers. Rather than it being too much of an experience, will it not be enough?

Nick and Pedro's plans to get Ayahuasca and go to Paris' land sounds more up my alley. I like pushing the limits, and that mindset carries over to my intentions with Ayahuasca. I don't want to have my hand held by a shaman who thinks I'm just another Westerner.

I am searching for the answers to life's big questions. I know they've all been asked before and I'm not unique in my curiosity, but I do have authentic questions. Questions about myself, my existence, life and love, and I want to know whether hedonism is a true path to happiness (which would lead to a more Epicurean lifestyle). These are the types of answers I hope to find, and I hope this spiritual, mystical experience will give me that.

I want to break free from the confined walls of my intellectual understanding. I want to tear down the blinders that are blocking my vision. I have tried my best to figure this whole life thing out, but I still don't get it. This is one of the last places I haven't looked. I've studied a great deal to get to this point, but now it's up to me to meet the medicine.

I'll *rendezvous* with Otillia outside my hotel tomorrow morning. From there, who knows what will happen next. Many people have had great things happen to them during great adventures, and I hope to be one of them—my adventure begins now.

CHAPTER SEVEN
NOW ENTERING THE AMAZON

MONDAY, NOVEMBER 5
8:52pm, Sitting in my hammock on Otillia's property in the jungle

This morning I met Otillia outside my hotel with all my bags. I got them into the back of the Motokar she arrived in, and we drove away from the hotel and into the one-way traffic circling around the plaza fountain. When we reached the other side of the plaza we went straight out of the city the same way that I'd come in.

"*Lo siento,*" I blurted out as I turned to her, "*no habla Espanol muy bien, es problema?*" She looked back at me with a smile, which made her dark eyes squint together and intensified the happiness she seemed to posses. Her eyes searched mine for a split second. "*No problema amigo,*" she said, then she leaned forward and explained the directions to our driver.

A couple minutes later, we pulled up to a small outdoor street market. She got out and, just like Luis, motioned that I should stay in the Motokar. She walked off with a certain kind of grace. Unassuming, yet assertive and sure of herself. I like those traits in someone who's going to be my guide.

She came back carrying two plastic bags that were filled with all kinds of groceries. I could see potatoes, apples, mangoes, broccoli, tomatoes, and a bag of rice. There were a few things I couldn't see, and I couldn't help but wonder if she also got some trippy jungle plants. I wasn't really sure how this whole shaman thing works.

After we had our supplies, we drove a few more blocks and were let out next to a ramshackle van/taxi depot. Both of these vehicles are uncommon here in Iquitos, which makes sense since a Motokar is much easier than a car to ship on a boat upriver.

I stood with my bags while Otillia organized our ride with the man running the taxi outpost. When she was finished with the negotiation, the man told me to put my bags down and led me towards an old Honda Accord. Another man opened the passenger door for me and I climbed in and sat in the front seat.

Otillia got in one door, and through the other came another older woman I'd never seen before. They sat down and exchanged a friendly, yet refined, greeting with each other. Turning around in my seat, I tried to understand what they were saying. Otillia introduced the woman as Juliana and I shook her tiny soft hand.

The driver got in and we departed from the depot down the only real road there was. We passed the military school and the airport and then the true rawness of the Amazon began to expose itself.

I gazed into the jungle and saw the most diverse variety of plants I'd ever seen. I was in awe at how many shades of green there seemed to be, and how many different kinds of plants I saw.

As soon as I'd gotten a look at one plant, it would pass by and be gone. Then I would see another plant I'd never seen before, and then it would be gone just as fast.

This continued the whole drive. We passed "retreats" that had big signs, single homes in different stages of construction, and lots of shacks that were always grouped together. We passed stands selling fresh *coco de holchada*, fruits, flowers, and bottles of gasoline for the Motokars.

I managed to exchange a few Spanish sentences with Otillia and Juliana during our half-hour drive, but I only understood the simplest phrases. Unfortunately, neither of them spoke any English, so my options were pretty limited—I either needed to learn more Spanish or I wasn't going to be able to communicate with anyone.

I told her I was from Canada and Otillia smiled back. "*Persona de*

Canada, bueno persona," she said. Now THAT I understand. People might not know of Vancouver, but some Canadian had already left a good impression on her.

It's nice to be proud of where you're from. The nationality you are born into is probably the most influencing factor fate hands a man in his life.

I was staring into the jungle, lost in my thoughts, when Otillia pointed out a sign with KM50 painted on it. Soon afterwards, we pulled over to the shoulder. The driver turned off the car and got out to help unload our bags.

We took everything and crossed the street, seeking refuge from the heat in the shade of a broken down, homemade bus stop. I got there first and put down Big Red before going back to help carry the bags of groceries.

Standing in the shade, I peeled my shirt off and waved it in front of me to dry it off. The fresh air felt soft on my bare torso and I sat down roof opposite Otillia under the palm-thatched.

Juliana walked up behind us but didn't sit down; she scurried off into the jungle. I turned and watched her follow a well-worn path and then she disappeared behind the dense foliage.

Otillia started speaking to me slowly, but I still had a hard time catching most of what she said. However, because she was using the simplest language she could, I caught a little. I understood her when she told me "*dos hombres*" were coming back to carry our bags for us. Carrying my pack and food probably wouldn't have been a problem but I was already exhausted from the heat and humidity and we hadn't even gone anywhere yet.

It was close to 2 PM and the sun was broiling anything it touched. I tried to hide in the small sliver of shade the broken palm leaf roof provided. It was clear this make-shift bus stop had seen better days.

I took a drag of humid smoke from my cigarette and tried to explain what I did for work (*trabajo?*)

"*Mi casa* is in California and I *trabajo* professional skateboarders," I said. "X-Games? Guinness World Record?"

"Trickas?" she asked curiously. When she looked down at the skateboard under my feet and pointed, I knew what she wanted.

Not one car had passed us since we sat down, so I got up and walked into the middle of the street. After a few kick flips and 180's up the street, I turned back and pushed full speed towards the bus stop.

Leaning forward on of my board, I wheeled past her on the front two wheels of my board in a manual. With lots of speed from the big pushes, I maneuvered my body back and forth to keep my balance. Out of the corner of my eye, I saw her stand up and take a step out of the bus stop to watch me fly past.

I made it 40, maybe 50 feet past her, but when I started to slow down I lost my balance. I was leaning too far forward and the nose of my board caught the ground and I got slammed forward onto the gritty asphalt.

Down for only a second, I jumped up right away to show her I was ok. It didn't really hurt when I pushed towards the bus stop, but the rush of adrenaline mixed with the hot sun made me feel nauseous. Sweat ran down my face at an impressive rate. I tried to inconspicuously look at the gravel and dirt embedded in my elbow, but I was too obvious, and she saw me inspecting myself. Of course she was a little worried, so I leaned back, hiding it from view.

Laughing, I smiled at her and explained I was all good. She was worried, but I could tell she enjoyed the show by her smile. I'd seen the look she gave me, mostly from my parents—it meant something like, "I love you, but you're crazy."

After close to an hour, the two men came out from the trailhead. I put The Mothership on my back and the two men grabbed the rest of our load. We all turned and walked across the small bridge that spanned the ditch behind the bus stop. We walked along a path with Otillia leading the way. I was behind her and the two men waited a couple minutes to give us the space to go ahead privately.

Across a clearing was a big lagoon. We skirted the edge of it and entered the jungle, then crossed a small wooden bridge that went over a tributary for the lagoon. We turned right, and after a few minutes the path led up a sloping hill.

Otillia pointed out plants and animal markings as we walked along. Even without saying much, I learned from her. I was in the heart of the jungle, walking along a path lined with piles of dead leaves. High above were long vines hanging from tall trees and the sounds of birds rang out from all directions. It was overwhelming.

The smells and sounds were as dense as the scenery. The smell of the fresh yet humid air was palpable, and I felt the power of being surrounded by it. Each breath tasted like a sip of the finest air I'd ever drunk. I was astonished by how much there was within the jungle's canopy; the immensity of the jungle ecosystem is truly unfathomable.

We walked for about 20 minutes and then descended a short hill into a big open clearing. The two Peruvian men walked into the clearing soon after carrying our entire load with grace and ease. Their skin shined with sweat when the sun hit them as they walked. Both were small men with taught muscles that bulged under their tanned skin.

Otillia gave instructions to the younger of the two men. One escorted me along a trail that went past the main house and up a hill to the center of the big clearing. At the top of the hill, I got a better view of the property. On the ridge of the hill were two small wooden huts, and at the end of the path was a larger, two-story building. The bigger building had an open balcony on the second floor. Beyond where the property had been cleared it was all jungle, dense jungle that looked like it was spilling into the clearing from all sides.

Below me on the ridge was the main house where Otillia lived and next to her house there was a small open-walled building. It had some picnic tables inside so I assumed it was where we ate. Further back, on the opposite site of the property there were two more small wood buildings and one building at the top of the hill that looked like it was still being constructed.

The man directed me into the first small house on the ridge and placed my bags inside the door against the wall. I walked in behind him and looked around my new home, or "*tambo*" as he'd called it.

The materials it was made from looked like they'd all come from the surrounding jungle. When I looked closer at the floorboards, I saw the lumber had been cut with a chainsaw, and every board had unique swirls where the blade had slid across it. Looking at the other beams and posts, I saw they were finished with the same technique.

The man motioned for me to follow him past a plywood partition to the right side of the house, which had a bed on one side and a toilet on the other. He showed me how to flush the bucket-powered toilet by dumping water from a plastic barrel into it.

Next, he pointed to where a few candles were placed under the table, and after that he seemed content to let me settle into my new home. As I watched him walk back down the hill, the sounds of the jungle seemed to get louder.

Later in the evening, after I'd had dinner, I decided to see Otillia in the main house. I was in South Africa a month earlier and bought some souvenirs for her, thinking she might appreciate gifts that came from halfway around the world.

I had an African shaker with a small swatch of zebra skin wrapped around the handle, a little drum with intricate African artwork, and a conch shell I found when I went to Cape Agulhas (the southernmost tip of Africa, where the Indian Ocean meets the Pacific Ocean).

I also brought a few types of American tobacco. I read that they use tobacco in a different way in the Amazon than we do in America. For the Peruvians, tobacco is used ceremoniously and with respect for the process of smoking. Research has proven the damaging effects from habitually smoking cigarettes, but I wondered if there could be physical and spiritual benefits with more traditional tobacco use.

When I went to see her it was dark, and the main room was lit by candles. We sat smoking, both rolling forward and back in rocking-chairs made from bent rebar and plastic straps. The candles seemed to be whispering silent secrets and playing with the shadows, and we went from having discussions to moments of peaceful silence. There I was, sitting in a Shaman's house, in the middle of the Amazon, (somewhat) communicating in her native tongue.

I thought about everything so far and I felt content. This was exactly the kind of escapade I'd been looking for. Putting the trip together had been so easy, and I never spent much time worrying about the challenges I would have to face. It was something I wanted to do and I went for it.

In the middle of our broken dialogue, Otillia laughed and said something about my Spanish being *"poco mas bien!"* She said this while shaking her head and laughed again when I told her, "Yo habla Espanol cinco dias." I'd only been speaking Spanish for five days.

Swinging in my hammock and writing, my page illuminated by candles, I'm repeating a light mantra: "*A swaying hammock keeps the bugs away.*" I say this over and over in my mind and occupy my body by pushing off the wall partition to keep myself in constant movement. Swinging gently from side to side creates enough of a breeze to deter (most) bugs from landing on me

One thing I'm worried about is how much it's going to cost to stay here. I haven't discussed it with Otillia, but I'm worried because the people from the Maripoza Center said they paid $2,500 for their 10-day retreat. At that rate I could afford a few days, but I want to stay for a longer, extended period of time. I like Otillia, and she has such a beautiful property. With her guidance I would like to do some serious spiritual and emotional work.

The jungle has an incredible amount of life and diversity. I expected the bugs and animals to be so loud they were intrusive, but it's not as disturbing as I'd feared. The symphony of the jungle is in fact, *perfecto, tranquilo*—I guess you could say this is just what I wanted, so far at least, but let's see how my first night goes.

CHAPTER EIGHT
AYAHUASCA, I CAME TO FIND YOU

TUESDAY, NOVEMBER 6
9:50am, my tambo after breakfast

I was reading in bed early this morning, enjoying the warm air on my bare skin, when I heard a knock on my door. I put my book beside my pillow and peeled back a corner of the mesh bug net to slither out through the opening. Tying the drawstring of my board shorts, I walked out to see Juliana. She gestured for me to come eat.

I grabbed a T-shirt and my book before walking down the hill through the wet morning grass to the building with the picnic tables. I guessed I was the only one around because the table was set with a complete breakfast, for one.

After pouring a cup of hot tea from the thermos, I started on the plate of scrambled eggs. I saved the best part of my meal for last, the huge bowl of freshly-sliced mangoes and massive grapes. I never knew grapes could be so big, the size of small apples, and the mangoes were as sweet as candy.

From my conversation with Otillia yesterday, I learned tonight will be my first Ayahuasca ceremony. I tried to eat as much as I could at breakfast since it will be my only meal today.

Now I'm back in my tambo and sitting in my hammock, filled with thoughts about last night. Between the animals, the bugs, the rain, the thunder and lightning, and everything in between, it was intimidatingly loud. The ambient noise was the buzz from the insects, and above it were the screeching birds and crackling thunder.

I survived my first night in the jungle and it was an experience I'll never forget, that's for damn sure. Tonight will be my first time drinking Ayahuasca. From what I've learned about this plant, and how it's used, I am ready to meet whatever experience I am given.

I'm ready to live,
I'm ready to die,
I'm ready to see.

I came across a quote in Plato's *The Apology*, from a dialogue with Socrates explaining that even though he'd been charged and condemned to death, he is not disturbed: "No evil can happen to a good man, neither in life nor after death."

I feel this relates to me now. If I believe I'm a good person, I must believe that no evil can happen to me, either now in life, or later in death—but we will see.

CHAPTER NINE
IT WAS THE DAY AFTER

WEDNESDAY, NOVEMBER 7
10:17pm, my tambo

Saying the jungle is amazing is like saying the Sistine Chapel is a masterpiece. In reality, they are both much more than words can describe, and the true essence of both can only be found through experiencing them. The jungle is God's masterpiece, a harmonious pièce de résistance, and at the moment my personal safe haven. On the other hand last night's Ayahuasca ceremony was painful—dreadfully, physically painful.

At around four or five o'clock I was reading the end of Plato's *Apology* when Juliana came to my tambo. She motioned for me to come with her and for some reason wanted me to bring my towel.

We walked down the little path towards Otillia's house in the late afternoon sun. Instead of going towards her house she led me to an area where there was a bathtub sunken in the ground. It was filled with water and all kinds of floating leaves and plants, and Juliana imitated getting into the bath and washing herself and pointed to me.

I nodded my head that I understood but couldn't help feeling shy with her standing there. She looked at me with a confused look. Was I supposed to get in the tub with her standing there? If so, should I get in naked? Or wear my shorts? Luckily, she turned away and I watched her scuttle back towards the house.

Looking around, I didn't see anyone, but I still wasn't sure of the customs, so I kept my shorts on when I slipped into the bath.

The tub was filled with a refreshing mix of green shrubbery, and these plants gave the water a slight cooling effect. I lay back in the tub, looking up at the blue sky, the colors of the jungle canopy rich in the golden hour of sunlight.

I closed my eyes and lowered my head underwater. It felt natural and my body released tension from deep within. I lay in complete tranquility for what felt like an appropriate amount of time, and when the sun was slightly lower I got out and walked barefoot up the hill.

On the path ahead of me were three new people who'd just arrived. Juliana was leading them towards the big tambo at the end of the path.

Turning off the trail towards my tambo, I went inside to change out of my wet shorts. I picked a few crushed leaves off of my back, put on dry shorts and a T-shirt, turned on my portable Nixon speaker, and played some music. Swinging in my hammock, I smoked a cigarette and listened to Billy Joel, singing along to the parts I knew.

Earlier, Otillia told me the ceremony would begin when it gets dark, and to come down to her house then. Before I went down, I felt like I did when I landed in Lima a few days ago; I couldn't tell if I was excited or nervous. *Who the hell cares*, I thought. There wasn't much difference between the two and I decided I had to stay open to whatever experience I get.

The dusk muted the colors of the forest and I lay in my hammock, swinging from side to side, waiting for the night to finish swallowing my diminishing view.

Before long, I saw two bobbing headlights approach me from the big tambo at the end of the trail. Three newcomers walked past me. They were talking in melodic and hushed Spanish. They continued down the hill and disappeared out of sight. I rolled out of my hammock, walked over to the desk in my room and grabbed my cigarettes, lighter, and bug spray from the table.

It was my first time using the heavy-duty DEET bug spray because it seems toxic. I'm taking my natural diet seriously and I want to detoxify and purify myself. Spraying myself with DEET is something I only plan to do before ceremonies. Today I counted 63 bites on my arms and legs, and that's just since I got here.

I turned on my headlamp, blew out the candle, stepped outside, and took a deep breath. When I began walking down the hill I started getting abnormally hot. A few drops of sweat trickled down my ribs and my arms and even my legs began to perspire. I wasn't sure if I was experiencing anxiety, but I didn't think that could be it. Or was it?

I walked into the main room of Otillia's house. She was sitting at the back of the room in her rocking chair and there were three large candles burning in a metal bowl in the middle of the room. They illuminated her big smile as I came into the light and I turned off my headlamp.

From the few meaningful interactions I'd had with Otillia, I was beginning to really like her. We had a natural connection which felt unique and special. Even without much verbal communication, I'd met enough people in this world to recognize a mutual understanding.

Cushions were folded and placed around the room for each of us to sit on. In total there were four seats. The guys I'd seen earlier had their backs against the wall to Otillias left. The third guy sat against the wall to her right, with an extra seat for me between him and Otillia.

The guy sitting closest to Otillia, on her right, I recognized from my first night in Iquitos. It was Radolpho, the musician who had been playing at the Karma Cafe. Next to him was a tall European-looking guy dressed in the latest hippy jungle fashion. He wore clothes and jewelry befitting of any spiritual jungle psychonaut.

The two guys on her left were both setting up little altars next to their seats. From what I could see, they consisted of stones, feathers, and other personal effects. The guy next to me was kneeling with his palms outstretched in front of him in a prayer position. Not wanting to interrupt, I silently examined the random items he'd placed beside his seat: a crystal, a book of some sort, a necklace, and a picture I couldn't quite see in the dark.

Juliana came out of the kitchen with five plastic bowls and placed them next to each of us. According to the stories I'd heard, these were for puking, or purging into. I'd heard all kinds of stories before this. They all said it was common to purge at least once during an Ayahuasca ceremony, so at least that part wasn't going to surprise me.

"*Hola, señor,*" Otillia said, looking past me at my praying neighbor. He raised his torso with a flat back and looked towards her.

"*Hola senor, este es el hombre del que te hablé. Él sólo habla Inglés así que por favor haga todo lo posible para traducir lo que digo para él.*"

"*Señora, no entiendo,*" he said back to her. I didn't understand myself, so I thought this guy must not be able to speak Spanish either.

"*Habla usted Inglés?*" She asked him.

"*Yo sólo hablo un poco de Inglés y un poco de Español,*" he replied.

"*Por favor, explicar en Inglés, para el Americano,.*"

"*Si señora.*" He nodded his head and then turned to me.

"Hell-O," he said, "My name Giovanni. I am Eeetalian."

"*Hola.* Sean, from Canada." I leaned over to introduce myself. He told me he was going to help translate what Otillia said into English for me, but to please forgive him as neither English nor Spanish were his first language. This was awesome news for me. I'd assumed I wouldn't be able to understand anything that was said during the ceremony.

He was being honest when he to me he didn't speak English very well, but it was still a relief to have some help. He said he was Italian and had been living in the jungle for the past six months. He was staying on the other side of the road in a place called the Rainbow Community.

I had heard about this commune-like camp from two guys I met in Iquitos. They had known about Otillia's but never visited. From what they told me, it sounded like there was a bunch of artists living in huts and tents—a little community only a few kilometers down the main road.

It was Giovanni's second ceremony with Donna Otillia, and he said his first experience was perfect.

And so it began. Otillia told us it was important to stay open and relaxed during the ceremony. She recommended setting a personal intention to focus on after drinking the Ayahuasca. It was all familiar to me because my friend Kari gave me the same advice when she told me about her Ayahuasca experience here. I had already thought about what my intention would be, and while I didn't have a fancy shrine I did have a piece of paper in my pocket with a sentence asking Ayahuasca:

Show me what I need to be shown.

I was still sweating, feeling like I was overheating. Otillia called me up and I kneeled before her. She poured Ayahuasca from a large plastic jug into a small wooden cup. I reached for it and closed my eyes. I said to myself *Show me what I need to be shown,* and gulped down the thick liquid.

It was absolutely disgusting, and so thick it coated my mouth and throat like mud. I imitated what Otillia had demonstrated and took a sip of water, rinsing out my mouth and spitting into the plastic bowl.

Fuck! Good thing I was a professional drinker in my past life, because holding down a shot of Ayahuasca was comparable to taking a big shot of absinthe. Gulp, burp, breath… *Come on,* I told myself, *you can do this!* It was harder to stomach than waking up to a tequila shot.

After everyone had taken their turn, Otillia took the cup and poured herself a shot. Bowing her head, she paused for a moment and then slammed it back. She gagged a little, then rinsed her mouth and spat into her bowl like the rest of us did. Putting the small wooden shot glass beside her on the floor, she stood up out of her rocking chair. Her white dress blew in the light breeze and she walked into the center of the room to blow the candles out.

I think we must have been sitting in silence for close to an hour before I started to feel physically uncomfortable. Shifting around in my seat, I tried to find a position which didn't hurt, but it was impossible. I gave up and stretched out flat on my back on the cushions. My joints were achy and sore, like I had the flu.

Radolpho began violently throwing up into his bowl. I am not sure which began first, but in between bursts of his explosive vomiting, Otillia began to sing in Spanish.

She was holding a tight rhythm with her "chakapa" she had shown me the night before. It's a shaker, or rattle, created from a bundle of leaves tied tightly together. Shaking it against her leg created consistent auditory stimulus for us to focus on.

Radolpho stopped puking and lay curled up and whimpering. *What the hell happened to him?* I thought. Otillia continued to sing and shake her chakapa and walked across the star-lit room towards him. She hovered over his crumpled body and sang a soothing song in Spanish while standing directly over him. "*Curacion, Curacion,…* something something…*Curacion…*" it was a pretty nice song whatever the words meant.

Next, I heard Giovanni start puking next to me. The smell of his large, sloshing deposits began to drift towards me and I fought the urge to puke myself. It didn't seem right to let his puke be the reason I puked. If I did purge I was waiting till the last second, when I was meant to on my own accord.

Fighting my stomach, I heard the guy next to Radolpho start puking, too. Radolpho puked again, and Giovanni was making some kind of growling sound, dropping small burps of slime into his bowl.

It was so gross I started laughing. *Seriously, what the hell is happening,* I wondered. The wildness calmed down after a while and Otillia kept singing. Before long I began to realize I was going to puke, but I didn't want to make a loud, embarrassing eruption in front of everyone.

Something I've come to know about myself is I prefer to be alone when I puke. Being an experienced drinker made this seem sort of ordinary, and not difficult at all. It reminded me of being outside a club and puking in the bushes before going back inside to continue partying.

When I stood up to walk outside, the light from the moon illuminated my path. I wandered across the small yard to where the clearing stopped and the dense jungle began. As I watched the dark contents of my stomach splash onto the grass, I began to physically feel better. I had a few good hurls and raised my head from my hunched position to look up at the starry sky.

Looking back down, I peered straight ahead into the pitch-black expanse of jungle. I began to see the "famous" geometric line-patterns, the ones that are often associated with Ayahuasca visions, coming out from the infinite darkness. It was beautiful; the intricate, mathematical patterns were very complex and well defined—but it wasn't what I wanted to see.

I was hoping for a big vision, but the geometric patterns made me think I wasn't having an original experience at all. I came into the ceremony having already seen and heard about the geometric patterns that people see when they drink Ayahuasca. I wanted original visions, and these could very well be impressions from my memories.

I walked through the clearing towards the sound of Otillia singing and stepped back into the ceremony. I felt refreshed after purging and when I sat down it seemed much hotter than before. It made me think of when I first came down to the ceremony and had begun to drip sweat. Why had I been sweating so much those first 30 minutes? It had subsided, but now it felt like it might be coming back. But this wasn't my skin that felt hot, this was something inside.

Everyone was sitting on their cushions, looking more peaceful than they'd been just a short while before. Otillia was sitting in her chair singing a rhythmic song, shaking her chakapa. She nodded to me when I sat down and tried to get comfortable in my seat.

When I lit a cigarette, my joints all hurt, my back hurt, my stomach hurt, and the feeling of peace I had walking in left me. I put out my smoke and lay on my side. My temperature was steadily increasing.

I started sweating more than I had before the ceremony. I could feel my shirt sticking to my body where it was saturated with sweat, and heat radiated outwards from my core. Drips of sweat fell sideways across my forehead and onto the ground from where it was resting on my outstretched arm. I rolled over so to look out the door and up at the stars that were scattered throughout the clear sky, trying to distract myself from what I was going through physically.

My fever suddenly broke after what was another painful hour or more. I sat up, thankful for it to be over, soaking wet and exhausted from having sweat so much.

Looking across the room at Otillia, I realized she had stopped singing and was lighting herself a Mapache, a large hand rolled cigarette made from jungle tobacco. When I bent my head forward to light myself another cigarette, I caught a glimpse of the written intention I had put next to me.

Show me what I need to be shown.

I wondered what the hell Ayahuasca was showing me. I leaned against the wall and looked around the room again. My vision was clear, my thoughts were clear, but my back, stomach, hips, and shoulders hurt.

"*Hola senores, como estas?*" Otillia asked us all.

"*Bueno!*" Radolpho said quickly.

"*Mas o menos…*" the guy next to him said in a subdued tone.

"Mucho grande visiones." Giovanni said next.

"Ah claro, beuno," said Otillia, "Es tu senor?" She directed her attention at me.

By this point I'd learned Giovanni wasn't much help translating my English, and not knowing how to explain my true feelings, I copied Radolpho to keep things simple.

"*Bueno, gracias.*" I said, throwing in the extra thank you hoping it made me sound calm and natural. Sitting there smoking, I realized I was beginning to get really cold. My pants and shirt were pressed against my skin where they were soaked in sweat, and when I extinguished my cigarette, I pulled my knees into my chest for warmth.

It didn't make sense. *Was it always like this in the jungle at night?* I thought. *Did it really get so cold? Should I have brought a jacket? No one warned me about this. How could I be so cold when I was just so hot?*

The temperature of my body continued to plummet and I began to shiver. I laid down in the fetal position and pulled my arms inside my t-shirt. I tried to use the cushion I'd been laying on as a blanket. I was shivering uncontrollably and I kept getting colder. I don't know how long this lasted, but the last half of the ceremony was brutal.

Otillia was still singing, but all I could think about was how cold I was. I was frigid and miserable laying there and tried to focus on Otillia's songs. By this point we'd been in the ceremony for at least three to four hours, and my back and joints were getting sorer each minute. I inched back into a sitting position against the wall again and hugged my knees close to my chest.

My body temperature eventually returned to normal and I was left there sitting in my wet clothes. In the warm jungle night, I was confused about what had just happened. Had it all been the Ayahuasca? Was I the only one this happened to? I thought.

The energy in the room began to level out and Otillia went around the room, singing a personal healing song to each of us, starting with Radolpho. She stood over us shaking her chakapa against the crowns of our heads, our shoulders, and down our backs. When she finished, she sung one last song to the group and then announced the ceremony was closed.

We all sat quietly until Radolpho broke the silence and asked Otillia a question about the ceremony. I tried to follow what they were saying, but I couldn't understand and soon lost track of the topic.

I collected my cigarettes, lighter, and the piece of paper with my intention written on it, strapped on my headlamp and said goodbye to Otillia and Radolpho. Their voices got swallowed by the sounds of the jungle as I walked to my tambo.

As for any kind of true visions, I don't think I had any during this first ceremony. During the four or five hours, most of what I remember is sitting silently in the dark room. Of course I thought about all kinds of things, but nothing I thought about seemed like a vision. It was more like daydreaming.

I don't really know how to feel about my first Ayahuasca experience. The physical discomfort was the most dominating part of it, and I feel more sadness within me today than yesterday. Hopefully this is part of the healing process. Hopefully this feeling is sadness leaving my body.

I guess when I think about why I'm here, it all comes down to one simple question, and it's the most important question I've ever asked myself. It may sound morbid, but it's an honest question that I need an answer to, and I came here to find the truth.

Is life worth living? Or, *what is the point of being alive?*

If I discover there is no purpose, and life is truly without meaning, then at least I won't worry about how hard I'm trying. It would relieve me to know there is an answer to this question, but above all else I want the truth, whatever that might be.

"More than love, than money, than fame, give me truth"

CHAPTER TEN
WHY AM I HERE?

THURSDAY, NOVEMBER 8
11:48am, laying in my hammock in my tambo

Yesterday morning I woke up and ate breakfast with the three guys who'd come for the ceremony the night before. They left after breakfast and I walked over to the main house to see Otillia. We sat across from each other in rocking chairs and smoked mini-Mapaches together.

I could hear Juliana in the kitchen filling buckets of water from the tank and shuffling back to the sink to where she was washing dishes. Otillia asked me about my experience in the ceremony. I brought my iPhone with me to help us communicate using the offline translation app Jabber. It's not always perfect, but it helped translate the key points I was trying to get across, and her Spanish is clear enough it understood what she said fairly well.

She asked me if I had any visions, but I told her I hadn't. She asked if it was a *bueno* experience, but I had to be honest and told her it wasn't really. It mostly just hurt, and part of the time I had a raging fever and then I had shaking chills. Both were intense and engulfed me.

She explained it was normal to experience these things. First, the medicine works on the *cuerpe* (body), and then it works on the

Espiritu (soul/spirit). For me to have experienced so much pain meant my body has a lot to heal. She told me she was going to bring me *un autra especial plantas medicina* the next morning.

Today I was awake, stretched out in my hammock, when I heard Otillia's footsteps swishing through the wet grass. I slid out of my hammock and said hello, and she handed me a small plastic cup. She explained it was the autra especial plantas medicina she had told me about the day before.

I smiled at her and took the cup. I'd slept well and was comfortable with this whole crazy jungle experience, more than before at least, now that the initial shock had worn off a little. I took a large sip from the cup and drained it.

She told me about this medicine last night. It's called Chiri Sanango, and apparently has many benefits. It stimulates the nervous system, muscles, joints and bones and energizes the emotions. It also helps in releasing trauma that has been stored in the body. At least that's what I understood from the translation my phone gave me.

I wanted to know if I was going to trip out, so I asked if there would be *visiones* with this medicine. She told me there wouldn't be visions, but my jaw may twitch, and my hands and feet might start to tingle like they were asleep.

A few hours later, the effects are exactly like she described them. It feels like I have pins and needles all over my body. My jaw is chattery, like I'm constantly shivering. My mouth and lips are numb, and my hands and feet feel like they were "asleep" and are waking up. Whatever that stuff was made from, the tiny shot of semi-clear jungle-juice has given me an interesting experience, not so much in mind, but in body.

I have been trying to sense what's occurring internally. In my imagination, I see small electrical impulses awakening and exciting my nervous system. It is as though my entire body is getting some sort of natural electro-shock therapy.

It is interesting that something organic can feel so non-natural. It feels electrical. I am trying to focus this electric energy towards refreshing my body on a cellular level.

Each day I am beginning to trust Otillia more and more. As I get to know her better she's also getting to know me more. Even without being able to fully communicate, I trust her sense of stewardship as she looks after me.

Whether sober, or in the middle of the ceremony, or prescribing jungle medicine like the Chiri Sinango, I feel like she understands me and wants to help me. To feel like someone cares as much as she does, it doesn't matter who they are. It is unique and appreciated.

Besides Ayahuasca, and now the Chiri Sinango, since I got here I've only drank water, natural tea, and the odd glass of freshly pressed fruit juice. The food has been equally pure, consisting mostly of fresh and organic veggies and fruits. The meals are prepared and served without a single spice, salt, or seasoning. While I wouldn't consider them the most mouth-watering meals, they nutritionally satiate me to the fullest.

The picnic table always has a large plastic thermos of warm tea sitting on it. When I looked inside it looked like fresh plants that had been growing on Otillia's land. It tastes a little weird but it's very soft and soothing. Surprisingly, it's nice to sip on in the heat.

If nothing more in my quest for health and happiness, this natural diet has been a great detox in itself. I feel closer to a state of homeostasis than I have in a long time. When I woke up yesterday I felt like shit, but today I feel much better both physically and emotionally.

Waking up without the pain and sadness I had yesterday makes me feel good about my decision to be here. The feelings I had yesterday morning slowly dissipated throughout the day and by the time I went to bed, I was feeling great. I never would have predicted that to happen when I woke up. I thought the whole day was going to be a write-off.

I'm beginning to think Ayahuasca really is healing my physical body first, just like Otillia told me. It makes sense: if you went to a mechanic to fix up an old beater car, the first thing they would want to check is if the frame's straight. Then they would work on the engine, and finally, they would focus on redoing the interior. Right now, I am aligning my body, straightening my frame, and the natural medicines are the mechanics at work.

Before my first ceremony, I was worried the intensity of the spiritual awakening might be too intense. I was expecting some kind of rapid enlightenment process that was severe and profound. It may sound contradictory, but at the same time I was also worried the experience wouldn't be as intense as I wanted it to be.

Perhaps it's true, maybe Ayahuasca is a physical agent that focuses on healing unprocessed traumas and the physical body first. I know I've had more than my fair share of physical trauma in my life—first as a ski racer, and then later a professional skateboarder (20+ fractures + a handful of surgeries).

I've also had enough emotional trauma from life-altering situations to know the taste of depression. One of the things I know I need to heal is the pain left in the wake of a horrendous year of marriage and subsequent divorce.

In my logical mind, I know that I have blocked myself from feeling romantic emotions because the body's defense mechanism after going through trauma is to numb itself.

There has been more emotional trauma than physical trauma in my life. Looking back on different chapters of my life, many of them seem clouded by a dark depression. It has taken me years to navigate away from the misdiagnosis of Bipolar Disorder, and many of the traumas surrounding those problems led to feelings of spiritual anguish. I've learned that as a man, I am abandoned here on Earth, solely responsible for the reality I create.

I can't help but think back to all the pain and suffering I put myself through with my shitty marriage. I haven't thought of her much since we split up last year, but when I do, I get angry with myself for making such a big mistake. I feel guilty too, because I know I let my family down. First by eloping with a girl I'd only known for one month, and second by being one of the few people in my entire extended family to ever get a divorce.

When we walked out of the San Diego court house, as Canadian man and Dutch wife, I thought the thunder that ripped through the sky was a good omen. It was one of maybe three times I heard thunder living in Southern California. The second was thirty minutes later as we consummated our marriage. I'm just glad I got out without getting her pregnant. The last I heard, she was remarried and already knocked up.

It's hard to forget these decisions because they're a reminder of my amazing capacity to make mistakes. The whole thing sounds a little crazy, even to me, but maybe being crazy has been my problem the whole time.

I had believed she would be stronger and wiser than the average woman because as a girl she'd had such a hard life. I thought she'd have more strength than the average American girl after overcoming the challenges she had to face.

The fact she had such a horrible childhood seemed like an obstacle which taught her amazing life lessons on strength. Nope, I was wrong about everything I believed to be true, about her, about myself, about love.

Something important I learned from the experience was that YES, it is possible to become stronger when faced with challenges in life, but only by facing and overcoming those challenges.

My ex-wife had been a direct hit, and in the war she fought as a child, she was bombed again and again. I fell in love with a young woman and it makes me sad to know it wasn't until later I found the young girl inside had been shattered. Unfortunately, whether it's the victims of a horrible childhood or the victims of war, sometimes people get broken.

I hurt myself most by trusting her words. She couldn't help it, and I never expected my emotional compass to misdirect me so far afield. I use my ex-wife as an example that I learned from first hand, but I am not judging or condemning her. She shouldn't have had to experience what she did as a child. It's not her fault, but it sure as hell wasn't my fault!

As much as I tried, we were never going to be a good match for each other and YES, I did learn that you should get to know someone for more than a month before asking them to marry you. At the time I was infected by the sick, manic fever of love. It wasn't authentic love, it was a distorted and insane love and I feel like a fool for allowing myself to be so illogical.

I believe it was our difference in upbringing. My mom and dad were always there for me when I got up for school and in the night when I went to sleep. It is a privilege that might be taken for granted by those who had it, and as I learned, unrealistically idealized by those who didn't.

The example my parents set of a loving relationship, and the way partners relate to each other, was way too different from hers. When the unprocessed traumas, the issues with her father (who I might as well just say, had been arrested with her in the car as a kid, shot her mom's ex-boyfriends, etc.), and the example made by her mother (who's in a long-term relationship with a married man), came head to head with the current reality she faced as a semi-successful model now past the age of 30, *and* trying to make a new marriage work with me. Add that all to the stress of moving from Holland to America while having to speak in a second language, and it was too much for her to handle. I can understand why, and I feel sorry for her.

When these issues became mixed with all my problems, of which there is no shortage, it became too much for either of us to handle. We argued, said hateful things, threatened to leave each other, and burned to the ground the temple of love we thought we'd built between us. I stayed with her out of a sense of duty hoping things would get better. They got worse.

I've always tried my best to be open about all the problems I have, but I learned that the reason people sometimes stay broken is because it's all that they know how to be. I may be foolish, but at least I'm honest with myself. It hurt to watch someone I cared about pretend they were ok, and yet suffer so clearly. I could never resign to that kind of unquestioning and stagnant life.

Intrinsically I have always felt forced to make myself better. As Nietzsche said, "I myself made myself healthy again..." And I knew it was up to me to reclaim my happiness.

Back when I first met my ex I thought it was noble to be with someone to help them be better, but it's not. I try to explain this in the chapter *Love & Loneliness* in "Beyond Ataraxia"—the book I've been working on. Here is the excerpt from that chapter.

"Looking back on my love affairs, and the people I chose to give my heart to, I realize I've always had the intention to somehow help my beloved. Whether it was helping them become a happier, healthier person, or by reflecting an honest opinion of how I saw them, I thought my honest perspective would benefit them. My purpose was to provide them with something they needed but somehow hadn't found themselves.

When I was in love I have usually felt that I could somehow bring out the best parts of my beloved. As though somehow they hadn't been able to do it themselves, but I could help them become that person. I wanted my lover to be their best. Nothing is sexier than potential realized, and I see so much potential in people, especially those I love.

Without the understanding I have now, I'd thought this was an honorable way to love someone. The problem is my immature ideas of love were ignorant. By striving to help my lover rise from despair I thought I was being a good lover, but I was not.

By defining love in this way I required my lover to be in constant a state of turmoil and disturbance in order for me to administer the personal charm of my so called "love." By wanting to help them rise, it meant they had to come from somewhere low.

It is the same with every charitable action. When desiring to help others it demands that there are others needing help, in states of disrepair. This works fine in health and medicine, but in love it's not a good practice.

There's a reason love isn't a popular topic among philosophers and that's because it's a topic better left to fools and poets. The ignorant and wordsmiths weave their tales and create mind-made fantasies which could never be possible on this earth, for they operate outside of nature's laws.

Real love is unthinkable, unimaginable, and can only be accessed through experience not thought. I should never want to help my lover, I should be a leader and find someone that in turn, I want to follow. In this way we help each other by helping ourselves. It's good to keep your head in the clouds, which is why I try to seek a clear connection with spirit and a higher understanding of my love, but I must not forget my feet. For now they are what hold me to this earth."

My ex-wife also left me a personal reminder that I'll have for the rest of my life. My right index finger is crooked, and the tip will always be numb from nerve damage.

She slammed it in a heavy, wooden door, and my finger *literally* exploded. That was the beginning of the end. Only a few months into our marriage, I knew in my gut it was over, but I invented many excuses to continue trying to make my marriage work. I wanted to be sure that when I looked back, I'd tried my best.

During that time, I was so poor I barely had enough money to feed us both. It was a struggle each month to pay the rent, and neither of us had health insurance. Sitting in my house after she slammed my finger in the door, I was speechless. I sat staring at my gaping finger, thinking about what options were available to me.

In situations that would make other people panic, my mind has always been reliable. No matter what injury, crash, or brush with death I've had, I find I get calmer, more focused, and even comical during the intense moments that follow. I guess it's a heightened "fight or flight" response.

I like being able to trust myself, knowing that no matter how intense a situation gets, my mind will stay calm.

I sat on the couch and asked my ex what the hell I was supposed to do? I started sweating from the excruciating pain. At one point I even vomited from the pain, something I'd never done before. I'd passed out, but never puked like that.

At a certain point, it became obvious that there was only one viable option: we had to go to the hospital. My finger kept getting more swollen, and it split open more and more until I could see the inside of my finger where the tip of the bone was clearly crushed. I was worried it could be worse than it looked and perhaps even worse than it felt. I began to worry because I thought I might lose my finger.

When I told my mom later that day that I had "accidentally" had my finger slammed in a door, she said, "Oh my, that's the first time anyone other than yourself has put you in the hospital."

And it was true, my poor mom has taken me to the hospital more times than any mother should, but it was always from my own actions. Growing up I loved to push the envelope in whatever sport I played, but I never got hurt by anyone other than myself. Here I was, the first time anyone had ever sent me to the hospital and it had been my wife who'd done it.

If only we could see ourselves as clearly as we see others. I'm able to analyze the lives of other people so much easier than I view my own. If only I could see my real problems, the seeds that my vices grow from.

Buried in my subconscious, there are parts that I hope Ayahuasca can heal.

This is not what I expected from Ayahuasca, I expected to "trip-out" more. I thought I was going to be shown things from an unknown spirit world. Secrets, which if there was a God, would have been intelligibly divulged to me. Through my heightened spiritual connection I would bring back tools for success to my personal reality.

Instead, Ayahuasca seems to be healing me in ways I didn't know I needed to be healed. Before I thought my physical body was strong and my spirit was what needed to be worked on. Now however, I'm not sure.

Ayahuasca does most of the hard work, I just sit there and reap the benefits. I read somewhere that one Ayahuasca session is equivalent to five years of therapy—it makes me laugh. Therapy is great, but it can be hard, and it is very slow and tedious. I'd much rather speed up the process.

With Ayahuasca, I am simply a vessel, a conduit, a flute through which the unknown can blow through to create harmony. I'd rather have the express version, even if it is more painful.

I do believe, and history will support this claim, that ingesting strong hallucinogens has the ability to expand what we consciously understand. They can even show us new truths about things we couldn't have conceived of before.

If the truth is what I see, and I don't see God, then for now, there is no God. I'm going with what I feel to be truthful, I trust Donna Otillia, and I trust nature.

I'LL HAVE A FRESH START

Chapter Eleven
PAINFUL PAIN

FRIDAY, NOVEMBER 9
6:15am, the large guesthouse with 8 bedrooms

It was 5:30 when I woke up—still dark enough to need a flashlight, but soon to be sunrise and my favorite time of day. I got out of bed and walked through the thick grass and up the stairs into the large guest house at the end of the path. More and more often, I've been going barefoot when I walk around the property. I'm not sure if it's safe, but I always prefer being barefoot if possible.

I climbed to the top floor of the guest house where there's a big open room and chose a hammock near the open edge. Sunken low and close to the ground, I watched the sun rise out of the canopy of the jungle. It sent laser rays of sunlight and one moment at a time I witnessed the world wake up. I felt energized and ready to start my day.

10:40am, my tambo

After breakfast, a man came to the property that Otillia called the "bone doctor." He was a kind old man who came to help me with the pain I've been having in my back. He gave me a unique style of massage and ended the session focusing on my twisted right index finger.

When I am at home, I don't like getting a massage from a man, but the bone doctor seemed to know what he was doing and I was able to relax. He didn't cure the pain, but he left my body feeling better than before.

After the massage, Otillia asked me to come with her. She took me to the tambo on the opposite side of her house and introduced me to a guy who'd just arrived named Joshua. He said he flew in from America last night and was planning to stay here for a few months to study the plant medicines with Otillia. I walked around the property with him and we took our time introducing ourselves and telling each other the story of how we got here.

He showed me where a section of the broken stream that weaves through the property was deep enough to bathe in. The stream was shallow and hidden in most parts where the bushes were overgrown. The watering hole is much better to bathe in than pouring buckets of water out of the blue plastic barrel next to my tambo. The water from the barrel is gross and smells like plastic, while the watering hole is refreshing and clean.

Tonight is my second ceremony, and I'm looking forward to it even if it is as painful as last time. It is necessary for me to face my most painful parts if I want to move past them. I accept the fact that if I don't allow myself to be chafed and polished I'll never be a clean mirror of reflection to my peers. If the wall of a house was cracked, you could fill in the crack only so many times before you'd need to look at what was causing the problem. I want to build a stronger foundation and straighten the parts that are crooked.

I have no idea what to expect in the ceremony tonight, but I feel cleaner than I did the first time. I'm hoping it will make the process easier.

Will I be able to relax and observe the process instead of trying to control it? Will there be anything to observe? Will it be as painful?

In the meantime Otillia, Joshua and I are going for a day trip. This afternoon, we are going to hike out of the property and catch a bus the last 50 km down the road to the town of Nauta. There, we will hire a boat to take us out on the Amazon River. I can't wait; Joshua said we might see pink-bellied dolphins!

5:50pm back at my tambo

We were drifting with the current in a carved wooden boat and had our eyes focused on the water, trying to catch a brief glimpse of the pink dolphins when they breached the surface. We had seen close to a dozen but they had been too quick to get a photo.

"*Es peligro?*" I asked our boat driver.

"*Mas o menos,*" the driver said, twisting his hand from side to side. When I stripped my shirt off and stood at the tip of the bow, Otillia and Joshua both laughed at me. I looked back at them and they had that look I know well: *I love you, but you're crazy.*

Fuck it, I thought, *maybe there's a massive Anaconda, maybe there's biting fish, maybe a parasite will crawl up my dick,* but none of it mattered. I wanted to be able to tell myself when I'm an old man that I'd swam in the Amazon River when I got the chance. I jumped into the warm, murky, swirling waters. The river was a chocolate color and dark below the surface. Today, and when I swam off the Southernmost tip of Africa are my two most memorable swimming experiences.

The ceremony was set to begin soon, and I was ready to dive in— headfirst.

Chapter Twelve

MAKING MEDICINE

SATURDAY, NOVEMBER 10
8:30pm, my tambo

When I woke up this morning, I was sore again. The sun was just coming up and I listened to the birds warm up their voices and find their harmony. Steam rose from the plants where the sun's warmth melted the night's wetness. And what started out dark lightened and the sad, painful, parts in me seemed to evaporate with it.

The sunlight becoming more intense and the day already heating up, I went and rinsed off in the watering hole, then came back to my room to write and find some shade.

I was lying in my hammock when I heard the crack of an axe echo through the jungle clearing. I threw on a T-shirt, brushed my hammock aside, and walked out of my tambo to see what was happening. There was a man standing with his back to me under the open-roomed building at the top edge of the property. I hadn't walked up to it yet because it was still being built.

When I walked up, I saw the man's coal gray T-shirt had a stripe of sweat running down the spine of it. Under the raised building, he had two small fires smoldering underneath two massive stainless-steel pots. From my online research, I knew he was preparing a batch of Ayahuasca, which meant it was going to be brewing for up to 24 more hours.

He was standing next to what looked like long branches and using the axe to split them into smaller, two-foot sections. When he was done, he piled the pieces on the ground next to a small blue tarp that had a rock holding down each corner. He sat down on a log next to one of the edges of the tarp and motioned for me to sit down on a log opposite him.

I hesitated to get closer, unsure if I was disrupting the Ayahuasca-making ritual. I wondered whether I was an impure gringo. *Do I have to be "cleansed" before sitting down (like when I have a plant bath before a ceremony)? Will the batch be tainted from my dirty presence?*

I thought about it for a second and then thought, *fuck it*. With a smile and an outstretched hand, I approached him the same way I approach every stranger.

"*Hola*," I said.

"*Buenos dias*," he responded.

"*Mi nombre es Sean.*"

"*Hola John, mucho gusto.*" He reached out his hand and introduced himself as Nino.

I sat down across from him on the log and watched him bash a two-foot section of thick vine with a stronger thick branch. His grin was filled with such perfect white teeth, you'd think he was raised by a dentist in the city, not a shaman in the jungle. After he'd smashed the section of branch about 20 times, its internals were torn open. Then he threw it on top of the blue tarp and the plant's nectar oozed from its tender meat.

"Ayahuasca," he said pointing to the chopped pile next to him.

"*Si.*" I nodded at him, the purpose of this mysterious activity now confirmed.

A flashback from last night popped into my head. After the ceremony, I had been walking up the hill and seen a fire flickering right where we're sitting now. There were the sounds of a man singing in Spanish, and it was gently wafting through the thick night air. He must have been making more than one batch and been here all night tending to the fires.

I wondered what would happen if you didn't brew it properly.

Maybe a bad trip? One thing's for sure, Ayahuasca couldn't taste any worse no matter how you brewed it.

I gestured and half-asked in Spanish if he wanted me to help him smash up the pile of vine pieces. Smiling back at me, he reached behind his seat and passed me a hard stick for me to use. I leaned forward and grabbed a meaty piece of vine. I noticed it was wet where it had been cut at the ends and was about three to four inches in circumference.

Imitating Nino, I started hitting the piece of vine against the log I was sitting on with another big stick and before long, we had the whole pile laying smashed to bits on the tarp between us. The emulsified pieces of vine had stringy pieces of bark hanging that looked fresh and juicy.

When we sat down for a minute to take a break, he wiped the sweat from his golden brow with his dirty sleeve and motioned for me to follow him. Standing, he bent down and split the pile in half. We transferred the two halves by the armfuls into the boiling cauldrons, the water instantly turning a slimy green. When we were done, he led me down the hill to where a small mound of shrubbery was growing beside Otillia's house.

As we walked through the grass, some of the deeper sections were still wet, and I felt the blades sliding through my toes as I followed him. He had been carrying two buckets and handed me one. The bush was big and leafy, to me indiscernible from any of the other big, leafy plants, but he said this plant was special, and tore off one of the leaves putting it in his bucket.

"*Chacruna, es especial plantas para Ayahuasca,*" he said.

"*Que nombre?*" I asked. "*Chacruna?*" I used my limited vocabulary mix with mimicking what he said to ask if that was the name of the plant.

"*Si,* Chaaaa-kkkkkkrrrrrruuuu-naahh," he said slowly so I could understand.

I repeated the word, and imitating what he'd done, I ripped a leaf from the bush and dropped it in my bucket.

"*Tres cientos,*" he said, picking another leaf.

I didn't understand, so Nino picked up more of the leaves,

counting them out as he went along, *"Uno, dos, tres…es importante para tres cientos."* He put down his bucket to clarify with his hands that he was saying three, three fingers and then two zeroes. *Ok, so we each pick 300 leaves,* I thought, *but why 300?*

At times I got lost on the specifics of our conversations. I tried my best to ask him about what we were doing now to prepare the mystical Ayahuasca brew.

"Chacruna y Ayahuasca es para Ayahuasca medicina, y visionnes? Si o No?" I posed the simple question, asking if it was the second plant that I knew must be added when making Ayahuasca. It was confusing because the vine had the same name as the finished product and that threw me off at first.

"Chacruna es luz," he pointed at the sun, *"Ayahuasca los plantas, esta curador, es para curacion y es professor de vida."* He pointed up the hill to where we had sat and smashed up the vine. Turning back to the bush he continued, *"Chacruna es para visionnes: mas Chacruna, mas visionnes."*

I thought about what he said thoughtfully. More Chacruna equals more visions, so no wonder some of the *gringo shamans* all offered "strong brews." It was easy: all you had to do was throw in some extra leaves. I was learning the name *gringo shaman* was synonymous with anyone who wasn't a local and makes these intense brews. Fittingly, there is an influx of tourists that want to find someone to follow as they hallucinate and trip out, and more of these shamans are showing up around here. God bless America…

In town, Raul told me that Otillia prepares Ayahuasca for more of a teaching/healing experience. Which makes sense, and I'm guessing that's part of the reason I haven't been gripped by intense visions. She must use a relatively small amount of Chacruna and more Ayahuasca.

Some of the other *gringos* I've met in town told me about some shamans, most of them white guys from America or Europe, who make crazy mixtures of Ayahuasca. They mix in things like mushrooms, cocaine, peyote, san pedro, or any number of other wild plants. They add this to their brew to make the trip more intense. Of course it gives a person extreme visions, but it isn't balanced and these shamans don't seem to give a fuck what the outcome is.

To me it seems irresponsible and unnecessary. As a drug, I've already learned how unique Ayahuasca is, and that it'll do what it wants, when it wants. That is why I believe it's important to have a shaman who you trust lead the ceremony.

I have faith in Otillia, and the way she prepares, and administers Ayahuasca. I believe it's more aligned with how indigenous people meant for it to be used thousands of years ago when they learned how to make it. I thought I'd need the strongest Ayahuasca I could find when I first got here so that I could have intense visions.

It made sense; strong trip equals more growth, right? However, I'm beginning to think that's not true at all. If I trust nature's medicine, and I trust Otillia, then I should use it in the way it was meant to be used. For some reason us *gringos* (foreigners) just love pushing boundaries. In a way, I feel like my entire soul is in the hands of the plant medicine, for that reason I respect its power.

Nino finished picking the 300 leaves before me and walked back up the hill. When I joined him, he motioned for me to dump my bucket of leaves into the second pot. It was bubbling and boiling with a green, frothy layer of foam on top. It looked like magic potion being brewed in a witch's cauldron.

We sat back down on the logs. It was cooler now that we were in the shade, and we took a break to cool down. When I offered Nino one of my last American Spirits, he exposed his bright smile once again and accepted my offer. I watched him light it and take a slow drag. He looked down at the burning tip of the foreign cigarette and took a second pull. It was a new kind of tobacco for him, from a different part of the world, and he'd never tasted one like it before.

"Muy suave," he commented and rolled the cigarette between his

fingers, looking at the American Spirit logo stamped onto the filter.

I smiled back and said, "*Si, muy suave.*" *Suave?*

The indigo smoke from our cigarettes drifted past our heads and blew away with the smoke coming from the fires under the pots. Watching it drift across the property, I felt happy. I hadn't been planning to help Nino prepare the Ayahuasca, but I'm glad I did. There was something about the process that brought us together.

As I sat there, I remembered seeing that the bottle Otillia poured our shots of Ayahuasca from last night was getting low. That must mean we'll be using the batch we just made soon.

Smoking the last of my cigarette, I thought back to last night's ceremony. It had been a progressive step in the direction I want to go, and a positive experience overall. It led me to the conclusion I'm not just to here to pursue a psychedelic journey; I'm here for much more than that. Ayahuasca is one of the means which will bring the true end I am here for, but there is a lot for me to accomplish before then. My purpose in the jungle is to find answers and heal myself. Already those are being given to me.

My purpose is to heal my body from years of eating a shitty American diet.

To heal the physical injuries I've accumulated from a decade and a half of skateboarding.

To heal my mental wounds from failed goals and deserted dreams.

And to heal the emotional wounds from my shattered relationships and loves lost.

Most people probably come here to do Ayahuasca because they're lost in their life and have no connection to their spirit. Contrary to what I thought before I got here, the healing I need isn't so much spiritual—for the most part my spirit is fine—it's all the other shit in my life that's the problem. In a way I already knew that.

Normally, the effects of a substance are relatable to the amount, or purity, which one consumes. However, Ayahuasca works differently than anything else I've tried. My second ceremony was a completely different experience from my first time even though I drank the same amount of Ayahuasca.

What makes it different from alcohol, pot, mushrooms, caffeine, cocaine, cigarettes, or any other drug is this: even though both times I had the same dose of Ayahuasca, from the same bottle, it was a totally different experience. It was so different, if I didn't know better, I would say it was a different drug.

I feel like a good person, but for God's sake, isn't everyone more or less a "good" person? I think we are, but the problem is that most of us are wrapped in cloaks of vice, and are ignorant about who we truly are. Maybe beneath those dark robes we are all filled with goodness, but I don't know.

The spirit I've been referring to is the essence of who I am. It is my character, my personality, my soul if you want to call it that, but most importantly it is who I am. I could lose an arm and still be me; I could win the lottery and still be me. It really doesn't matter because this part of me, my spirit, is unchanging. It is the intangible, an immaterial part of *me*, and this is what I will call, for lack of a better word, my spirit or soul.

Part of the reason I wasn't scared the first time I took Ayahuasca was because I already knew this. I want to continue to learn about myself. I don't know myself as well as I could, but I know that who I am is nothing to be scared of.

The intangible: it's what ties all humans, plants, animals, and binds the entire universe together. It is the reason things work out the way they do in life. Everything is connected and we are all one. The body is just hunks of meat and bone but the brain is like a computer. With an incredibly elegant design, it controls our operations. But who is the individual, who is the "I" and where does the essence of who I am come from? I really can't say, but I know it's the part of me that is my true self.

If there is any spiritual guidance I need, it's how to be more confident when facing the anguish and despair that overcomes me as a single individual cast out into the world.

If I think about the first ceremony, all I remember is how painful it was, like getting run over by a truck. The second ceremony hurt my body less and I didn't get a fever or the chills like the first time, but it still hurt.

When I walked into the main room and sat down, I started heating up again. I started sweating profusely for no real reason and my skin felt like it was on fire. It went away after 20 minutes or so, but I was left wondering why I had such weird heat flashes at the beginning of both ceremonies. *Am I nervous and I don't know it?* I thought.

I sat there in the dark room in the middle of the jungle, in the middle of the night, listening to the shaman sing for hours on end. My mind wandered and I thought about all kinds of crazy things, but it seemed more like I was daydreaming than tripping out. I felt like at any point in the ceremony, my sober mind could interject.

I felt like I was about to fall asleep. Lying there, my mind slipped into a state somewhere between waking and sleeping. Immersed in my thoughts, it was like half of my brain was creating thoughts and the other half was observing them.

Whether or not these were "visions" I don't know, but I remember thinking *Otillia is here to help me heal and make my time here less difficult.*

—There was a point later on during the ceremony when I knew I was going to purge. I felt like I was being guided outside and went to the edge of the clearing where it met the jungle and puked. Drenched in moonlight and bright stars, I saw the vomit as part of the darkness that lived within me. I was purging the darkness that was stuck and needed to be released—although that could have been just a borrowed notion, like the geometric patterns. I went back inside and lay down again.

I was on my back, arms by my side, when I imagined a medicine lady with buckets of plants coming out of the jungle. My body was opened up, split down the middle with my ribs pulled back and my chest cavity spread apart. She kept filling me up with buckets of plant medicines.

Later, as I lay on my side in the fetal position, my back sore, I imagined pain and darkness pouring, oozing, and shooting out of my back. An unfathomable amount of darkness rushed out from each of my lungs, and out onto the floor behind me. For a long time it kept pouring out of my back, and as it did the liquid coming out became cleaner, and my back began to hurt less.

I am here to break some of my old habits, some of my *bad faith* as Jean-Paul Sartre called it. As an adult I have never felt as clean as I am right now. The nagging voices that speak on behalf of my vices are less obtrusive than usual.

"Would you like a cigarette?" my mind asks.

"Yes, but not right now, I'll have one later..."

Maybe it's the organic fruit and veggie diet combined with the fresh rain forest air. Or, it could be the plant medicines. Whatever it is, I feel a sense of somatic tranquility.

Chapter Thirteen
GONE FROM THE JUNGLE

SUNDAY, NOVEMBER 11
7:30am, my tambo

It was 6:05 AM when I woke up and looked at the time on my phone. This seems to roughly be the time my body wants to get up each day. It may seem unusual to people who like to sleep until mid-morning, but for me it feels right. My limbs and muscles feel fresher than yesterday; my body feels great.

I just came from eating breakfast, and I'm waiting for Otillia or Juliana to bring me my morning dose of Chiri Sinango. We agreed that I would work with this medicine again today and I now know what to expect. It makes my mouth numb, it gives my body pins and needles, and it somehow feels like it's refreshing my nervous system.

It may sound insane to be taking an unknown jungle medicine, and it probably is, but Otillia suggested I take it again and I trust her. She believes it is "opening my emotions." I have faith that she's right. Even as I'm writing, I can feel myself feeling in ways I forgot were normal.

When I got here, my heart and soul were blocked, but now they've started to take deep breaths of emotion. Every healthy animal has a balance of healthy emotions, and turning my feelings off hasn't help me.

Let me explain. The feelings I have aren't manic, or grandiose, or overpowering—in fact, I feel nothing but melancholy. But I'm *feeling*. One of the emotions I *feel* has a large void surrounding it— love. I miss love, I miss waking up next to my lover as they sleep peacefully, kissing their neck, smelling their hair, touching their body, pulling them closer. I miss loving and being loved. I have experienced the sweet and tender kiss of Cupid. I want that again.

Kelsey, you have been in my thoughts every day and I think of you now. I'm scared to give you my heart because in the past it hasn't worked out well for me. Can I handle the rawness of love?

I am wary about whether you and I are meant to be together. You're so affected by the environment you grew up in. And the way your parents split up must have been so tough on you and your brother.

If there's one thing about you I know, and I'm attracted to, it's that you're a survivor. Since we met all those years ago, I've watched you rise to meet every challenge you've faced, and you've come out stronger.

You also have so many people that are shitty influences in your life. I've watched your friends use you, taking advantage of what you have to offer. I hate that and you deserve better. I hope you'll travel more, and by changing your geography you'll remove yourself from these influences. You deserve someone who cares about you.

If I were with you, I'd ask your opinion on the topic of love. How have you faced the emotional grief from your parents' divorce, or did you run away from it all? How have you learned to relate to your partner with communication and respect? The fact you were raised in Southern California, a moral cesspool in my opinion, makes me want to learn more about you before getting too attached.

That being said, you have been my muse for long enough that I can't stop myself falling for you more and more. I want these feelings to grow and I want to learn more about who you are. I desire you fully, and I realize now how much my affection is growing.

Despite having some obvious problems in front of you, the inner joy you emit is beautiful. Your optimism and energy is contagious, and I can barely think about you without getting turned on. Then there's the dedication which drives you each day, and the hope that motivates you—that's what draws me to you the most.

Another thing I love is when it's just the two of us and we're sharing our quick-witted, often ironic sense of humor. You have a charming laugh and you always get my jokes, no matter how dumb.

I have the prayer flag tied to my backpack that you gave me after you came back from Thailand. I have travelled with it all over America, Europe, South Africa, and now the Amazon. It makes me feel like a part of you is always with me.

On Friday, I untied it from my bag and brought it with me into the ceremony. I set it next to me like I saw Radolpho and the other two guys do when they set up little shrines during the first ceremony. This ceremony, I did the same with the Thai flag. I put a piece of paper on it that had my intention for the ceremony written on it.

During the ceremony itself, I felt exposed, alone, and lonely in the dark room. The mysterious world of my subconscious became interlaced with my conscious awareness. Having the flag next to me reminds me of Kelsey, my young beauty. It's as close as I can get to bringing my darling friend with me.

I went down to Joshua's tambo to chat. He has an entire corner of his room filled with candles and idols from different religions. It's quite an impressive altar and it's incredible he travels with so much stuff.

I'm glad there's someone here I can speak English with. When Joshua speaks, he takes his time, and always seems to choose his words wisely. There are things he talks about or shows me, like the sacred geometry made from pipe cleaners, about which I don't care too much. On other subjects, he's quite wise and I enjoy our philosophical discussions.

He came here last year and lived for five months with Otillia. The reason he's here now is to continue his apprenticeship, and learn more about how to use the different jungle medicines. Joshua explained many of the natural remedies and medicines that Otillia has growing on her property. The list was extensive and it made me think about how the jungle is like a pharmacy and Donna Otillia the prescribing doctor.

The more I get to know Joshua, the stronger our friendship becomes. In many ways he's my antithesis, but that might actually be the best part of our dynamic. Where I am dark, he is light, where I have seen, he is blind. True wisdom requires a broad scope of interpretation, and our differences complement each other. I respect his wisdom, and I think he respects my intellect.

Joshua is heading back into Iquitos after lunch and I think I'll join him. I want to get two big jugs of drinking water, and some snacks I'm allowed to eat on the Ayahuasca diet. I do get three meals a day here, and there is water, but I'd like a bit more. I'm trying to drink 4-5 liters a day since I sweat so much in this heat, and I should eat more because I think I'm beginning to lose weight.

Also, I'm running out of tobacco. My carton of American Spirits ran out a few days ago, and I am almost done the last pouch I kept for myself. Maybe I shouldn't have been so generous the first week I was here. I must confess though, there's no denying the main reason I want to go into town—I want to call Kelsey.

She turns me on so damn much, and I would love to hear her voice. I'm starting to miss her. Our recent adventures together are special memories, and more than anything it brought us together as really close friends, which is something I didn't think was as valuable as I now feel it is.

Last year, I traveled so much for work that I decided to move out of my house. Since last May, I've been living out of my backpack. My dirtbike, snowboard gear, library of books, etc., are in a storage locker. Whenever I'm back in California I stay with Kelsey, and over the last year we've spent every waking moment together when I'm home. It's pretty nice having someone that's looking forward to you coming home.

If your only experience with roses was looking at them grow in a garden outside a window, you'd love them as much as you could, but you wouldn't know their true essence. For that reason when they were gone there'd only be a slight sense of loss.

Yet if someone gave you a vase filled with freshly cut roses, and you saw how beautiful they looked up close, and you smelled their rich, heavenly scent, and you touched their silky petals, then you'd know them well enough that when they were gone you'd miss them.

For now I have no vase and no roses, but at least I know how beautiful my vase can be once I refill it with flowers. Most importantly, I'm aware that where once I was full there is now an empty space. It brings me peace to feel what I'm missing. I know how magnificent a rose can be and I want Kelsey to be my rose.

Yesterday Otillia told me that my emotions were asleep when I first got here. She said now they are beginning to awaken. I can see why she thought that; my attitude and energy has changed remarkably since I got here and she sees this each day as I become happier.

It's good that my emotions are awakening on all sides of the spectrum. Lonely, happy, sad, and excited: it is almost overwhelming to feel so much again after only feeling two emotions for so long. I've either felt like I needed to escape, or needed to keep fighting. It's been a long time since I felt anything more meaningful than that.

It's been like this for years, even more so since my marriage began, which by that point was already the beginning of the end. I feel like I was capsized and now I'm finally righting myself.

6:30pm, the Green Track Hostel

To explain a little more about my experience with Ayahuasca, I'd start by saying it's different in every way from what I was expecting. I was certain I'd come here and drink the murky jungle-brew and see the answers to life's greatest questions. I thought these answers were somewhere in a world beyond my conscious reality, in some kind of spirit world outside of the world we live in.

There's still a chance that our reality is separate from this "spirit world," but I doubt it. For those that believe, it's the place where God lives. For naturalists, it's the connections in nature, for anyone with spiritual awareness it's the unknown and infinite light, and for scientists it's the space between the atoms.

What I've found is our reality isn't separate from this spirit world I fantasized about. It is one and the same. There is no duality. There is no spirit world outside of us where God resides.

This means there are no universal answers to uncork, and the infinite wisdom I'm looking for is within and all around me. So far, the answers I've found haven't come down from heaven; they have arisen from within me. They were within me all along, but I had to give them my attention before I could see they were there.

The pain of letting go is part of the healing and detoxifying process. This chronic pain, which I didn't even know was affecting me, is starting to disappear. Now when I get up I feel different, I feel like I have better communication with my limbs which makes me feel refreshed, younger and more coordinated than before.

The next step with Ayahuasca, I hope, will be to work on my mind and nervous system. Once my body and mind become realigned, then the medicine can work deeper. It will affect the parts of my soul, my character, my true nature, which need attention.

When I say my body feels better, it's not because there's been an addition. It's the opposite. I've left behind a bunch of unneeded shit and I'm feeling good because of it. My beautiful, creative, fun-loving self is rising from within me.

When I flipped the page to finish writing that last paragraph, I was greeted by a single word:

Humility

I'd forgotten when I first got this journal, I wrote random words across a dozen or so pages. My thought was I would flip to a page, like I just did, and be inspired, or forced to think about the word I saw.

What does humility mean to me? For me it means an honest understanding, and expression, of your personal limitations. Knowing

RESTART & DETOXIFY

CHAPTER FOURTEEN
TOILING WITH TOOLS

MONDAY, NOVEMBER 12
8:30pm, Green Track Hostel

Part of me worried I'd lose it all once I came back to Iquitos. I was scared my vices might awaken and take control, but they didn't. At least not as much as I'd expected them to. It reminds me what it's like to be me and it's a good feeling.

Today in Iquitos, I skated around the bustling jungle city searching for plumbing parts. I want to improve the water/plumbing system in Otillia's main house. She has a 250-gallon tank that collects rainwater from the roof and I want to make it easier to have access to that water.

As it is right now, there's a large hose that leads from the tank to a single faucet. The faucet has a big red lever that you pull to turn the water on or off. It's the kind of faucet you'd normally use to attach to a fire hose. It is set a few feet from the doorway that separates the main room from the kitchen.

Sometimes when Juliana pulls the lever too far, the water comes out in a burst and the bucket gets ripped from her hands. Then when she's washing laundry, she has to go back and forth from the kitchen with buckets of water that splash all over the kitchen floor.

With a little ingenuity, I'm pretty sure I can make it better. I plan to attach a splitter to the faucet with two hoses that each have individual faucets. One will go to the sink so Juliana can wash dishes, and the other hose will go under the floorboards to the area outside where she does laundry.

Joshua and I went into town together and spent most of the day talking. He's quite an intriguing person. His eyes are solid brown with dark pupils and they always look dilated. It's hard to tell where his black pupils begin and the chocolate color ends. When he speaks, his voice is humble without ever sounding over-excited, and rarely do his words betray him.

He grew up on America's East Coast but now he's somewhat nomadic. From his stories, I learn he has visited many countries and studied with all kinds of different teachers on his path towards self-improvement.

I had already planned to go to check out the Green Track Hostel. Joshua was going to a place called Alfert's Hostel. It sounded like a good deal for a private room and I might check it out next time, but after being alone at Otillia's for so many days, I wanted a hostel with other backpackers to have a more social experience.

I told Joshua I would meet him later in the afternoon, at a place he knew called the *Vegetariano Restaurante*. Last time Joshua was living at Otillia's, he befriended the family who owns the restaurant. He would eat there every time he did what we're doing now, coming into town for supplies, once or twice a week.

At 23, their son is close in age to Joshua, and studies health and nutrition at a university in Iquitos. We invited him to join us while we ate lunch, and his mom prepared the three of us the *menu del dia*.

With Joshua's help, we started to have a slow, but easily translated, conversation. The son told us that people in his class, and even his teachers, don't believe he eats a strictly vegan diet. They don't think a vegan can be healthy and active like an omnivore. It is ironic that even the people teaching nutrition have this view.

I might have believed the same thing a few years ago. However, people like David Zabriskie, an American cyclist who completed the Tour de France on a vegan diet, have proven it's possible to be a vegan and thrive in life, even if you're an elite athlete. Science has proven that meat is less important in our diet than we previously thought. Good quality protein eaten at the right times is necessary, but not necessarily meat.

The streets of Iquitos become slow and lazy in the late afternoon. After lunch, I caught up with my new amigos, the group that Oscar hangs out with, young locals who sell bracelets and necklaces to tourists in town. I'd seen them while skating around.

Today, they were sitting outside the Karma Cafe. I skated up to them, and they watched me between attempts to sell their jewelry. They cheered when I landed tricks off the curb, but I couldn't last long in the heat.

After a few minutes, a lady across the street, in the upstairs patio of a restaurant, cupped her hands to her mouth and shouted to us. Unable to understand what she'd said in Spanish, I looked over for a translation from Oscar, my main contact in the group, and the first local I met here.

The lady said her son loved skateboarding and was asking if she could pay me to teach him a lesson. I looked over with a smile and gave her two thumbs up. Then her teenage daughter, who had been sitting next to her mom, came down from the restaurant into the street. She turned and walked quickly towards the plaza to look for her brother. Once she found him and brought him back, I could see he was shy and a little nervous. I slowly realized that me being a gringo was probably the strangest part about this whole situation.

I explained it would be better to go somewhere free from traffic and suggested we go to the end of the street. We walked down towards the promenade with Oscar interpreting our conversation as we went.

The promenade was busy. Most of the people around were locals, but a few tourists were easy to identify due to their height, light hair, new clothes, and many other tell-tale signs.

Pointing towards a spot under a large tree that had some shade, the young boy followed me and we began our skateboard lesson. The first thing I taught him was how to stand on the board correctly. Then we covered the basic skills, such as which foot to push with, and where to place your feet for an ollie (the trick when you jump in the air with the board).

As I taught him, a small curious crowd gathered. We spent close to 20 minutes practicing together, (or an hour, or ten minutes, or who knows how long, in this heat I get delirious) and when we finished he grinned at me. I congratulated him with a big high five when I could tell he'd absorbed as much as he could for one lesson.

He gave me the type of grin only a kid can give and the true kind of smile that comes when you've been sweating and laughing. There's nothing more honest than that look of happiness.

The boy was even happier when he saw his mother walking down the street from the restaurant. She had watched him, but he wanted to show her again what he'd just learned. He was quite proud of himself, and after we'd said goodbye to each other, he looked up at me with admiration. I nodded with respect and told him to keep skating his whole life.

I threw my board down and skated across the street. After a final kickflip I hopped off to sit down next to my friends. When I looked up from lighting a cigarette, the mother was walking out of the restaurant with a pizza and a bottle of water.

She smiled, showing off two big dimples in her cheeks, clearly proud of her son and grateful that I'd taken the time to help him. It wasn't just about gaining skills on a board, and I knew that, it was about being inspired, letting the passion of youth spill out of him. I'd given him something to stay up at night thinking about, and hopefully his mom would continue to support him.

I accepted the water she offered me automatically. In this heat, I pour sweat like an open tap. I told her I was on the Ayahuasca diet and couldn't eat the ham and cheese on the pizza. She understood and asked if I wanted something else. I told her that it wasn't necessary. I planned to give the pizza to my friends.

As I gave it out piece by piece, each one of them turned to her and said thank you. She could see her gift was fully appreciated and she thanked me again before going back to the restaurant.

We sat on the curb watching the sun dip over the Amazon River. I felt grateful to be me, and to be in the middle of such a wild adventure. I left my friends to their half-hearted attempts at selling jewelry and roamed around the streets at dusk.

I ran into Paris, the girl from Kentucky I met on my first night in Iquitos, while I skated. It was funny; she told me pretty much the same story Joshua had just told me at lunch.

The last time Joshua was here, on the day he was leaving, Paris was arriving in Iquitos and they happened to meet each other in passing at the airport. What can I say? It's a small airport and I guess they felt a spark between them.

Unfortunately, in their haste, one coming, the other going, they forgot to exchange contact info. Like two ships passing in the night, they had both hoped that one day they'd see each other again. They thought it would probably be in Iquitos, and somehow I ended up being the connection which reunited them.

I told her I'd been staying with an American named Joshua, and that he had told me he knew her. She was glad to have run into me and wanted to know how she could get a hold of him. I didn't know where he'd gone after lunch so I asked if she wanted to join us for dinner tonight.

At dinner, like many others I've seen, Joshua seemed drawn to Paris. Maybe even more than others. Personally, I don't have any sexual interest in her. She reminds me of a sister more than anything. But even without lust-filled desires, I can see that there's an attraction which draws people to her.

Joshua seems blinded by this attraction to Paris. I could see she had become the victim of his obsessive love. He told me before she got to the restaurant that he felt like the heart of his true love was getting closer to him. *Blaaahhhhkk*—it made me want to puke in my mouth because I knew this sickness from experience. He's not in love; he's in love with his idea of love.

We paid our bills and then the three of us walked together along the sidewalk towards the promenade. The evening air was cool, and carried by a light breeze, it danced around us.

When we got to where the street met the boardwalk we stepped over the railing onto a grassy hill. For a while we just sat and talked, then Joshua came up with the idea to lead us through some breathing exercises.

Paris and I stood up and followed his instructions. It wasn't the most relaxing way to digest a meal, but I'm always up for learning something new. The fire breath, I learned, was not meant to be relaxing. For five minutes we sucked in air and blew out our breath as hard and fast as possible. My heart was racing by the end of it.

Joshua impresses me by how much commitment he has to his health and development as a human. Every minute of every day seems to hold some purpose for him. I envy that. At home I'm lost in my little world, and it takes all I've got to be aware of the things that are affecting me. It's far from the proactive dedication that Joshua displays.

When we were done, I was good and sweaty (like most of the time in this area). I said goodbye to Joshua and Paris and walked alone through the quiet streets back to my hostel. I kicked rocks along the side of the road and said hello to feral cats and dogs who looked up at me from dark corners of the sidewalk.

Both of my hands always end up dirty at the end of the day. No matter what I'm doing, they always seem to get dirty.

The table I'm writing on is in the back courtyard of the hostel. It wobbles slightly and I couldn't fix it even though I tried. The sound of the rain is thick and steady on the umbrella above me. The light comes from a single bulb strung on a cord above my head. It is soft, and yellow, and it makes the pages in my notebook look inviting.

Many of my vices and cravings have been less intrusive today. Except the craving I sometimes get for an ice-cold Coca-Cola; that's at the top of my list. It's just the sugar I want, I see that now, but it's an addiction I never thought about before this trip.

This afternoon when I checked into the hostel there was only one guy staying in the dorm room they gave me. I didn't know at the time who it was, I just saw a big blue backpack next to a bunk that had a guy passed out on the top bunk. His face was turned away from me and his long hair covered the back of his neck.

Just now, when I went up to the room to get my notebook, the guy was awake. To my surprise it's Nick! The American I met when I first met Paris. He was packing his bags and we talked for a little while about his time at Paris' property where he'd just been staying with Pedro. He said they had gone really deep into the medicine and Pedro got a little freaked out and decided he wanted to go home. His new canine friend is going home with him.

Tomorrow Nick's going to meet a guy and buy more Ayahuasca, then he's going to return to Paris' on his own. His plan is to stay there for a week and totally involve himself with the jungle and the medicine. He's a true character and he's on one hell of a mission. I hope to see him again.

CHAPTER FIFTEEN
SEX, THUNDERSTORMS, AND FASTING

TUESDAY, NOVEMBER 13
11:30, The Karma Cafe

When I rolled my face off the musty pillow, the first thing I thought about was calling Kelsey. I miss her, I like her more and more each day, and I wanted to hear her voice this morning.

The Karma Cafe wasn't open when I first got to town so I had to go to The Dawn of the Amazon, the other *gringo* restaurant with Wi-fi in Iquitos. It didn't matter where I went, though, because Kelsey wakes up with the sun just like me. It's one of the things I love most about her. I knew she'd be up or getting up soon—unless she'd stayed out all night partying. It is Tuesday, but anything is possible with that girl.

She answered on the third ring, and was happy to hear me. It was cute and it felt significant to have my affection reciprocated. It made me miss her.

I'd take a girl who desires me for the right reasons a million times over what you'll find in dark bars on dark nights. Up until now, she's also kept her distance. It hasn't been all me. We've both been hesitant about letting ourselves get too attached, her less than me. I've proclaimed my singularity more than once, but now I'm realizing I truly care about her. I care about what happens to her in life, and I want her to be happy, but most of all, I want her to be my girl.

The feeling is a little scary to be honest, but I'm ready to put myself at risk again. I want to let my feelings continue to grow. *Fuck it.*

In many ways it's a new beginning for me, which by default, should bring me a new kind of love and relationship. My feelings are becoming cleaner. Now that they've had a chance to detoxify, they are becoming closer to their natural state.

Part of the reason I've kept my heart so reserved is because I've been reacting to all the shit that happened between me and my ex-wife. Back then, I'd loved without hesitation, giving my heart completely. That's the most valuable thing I lost in that relationship: my undiluted innocence.

I'll be coming to the table as a new me, someone much different from who I've been in all my other relationships. If I have a new respect for love, then it stands to reason I will have a new outcome.

After I called Kelsey, I finished my cold breakfast and went to the Karma Cafe to finish some stuff I had to do for the website. I sent a few proactive emails, hoping I'd get responses when I come back into town in a few days. After I charged my phone, I left and walked down the street to the promenade.

I followed it until it ended, and then continued to the Belen market for the first time. Before I got there I was hit by a heavy, pungent mixture of foul odors. I smelled the market before I saw it, and it's the smells I'll remember most. The stagnant air was probably close to 100 degrees, and the scent from the chicken carcasses, fish filets, pigs' legs, cows' tongues, and piles of vegetables and fruits flooded my lungs.

My hearing was the next sense I become aware of. The sounds of children laughing, women chatting, men dealing cards, street dogs yawning. The Spanish being spoken everywhere sounded like music. On top of that, loud music came from each street corner out of huge speakers.

It became a medley of noise as wild and foreign as the sounds of the jungle were the first day I got to Otillia's. Only after I got used to the noise did I get a chance to look around.

The market is a trading hub for so many villages and it looks like it has every conceivable item the jungle produces. I walked through the middle of it which at any given point was three to four blocks wide. The most interesting part was the infamous "Shaman's Alley." They were selling every kind of potion and plant you'd ever need.

But my favorite vendor was a short old guy, standing at one of the corners. He was directly in the middle of foot traffic, selling fireworks out of a plastic garbage bin. I couldn't help but stop. The excitable old man helped me fill a shopping bag and our eyes were equally childlike in their excitement when he showed me the different types.

I bought a whole arsenal of rocket-propelled explosives and planned to put on a fireworks show at Otilia's. I bought Juliana a gift as well—red and white nail polish, the colors of the Peruvian flag. For the two guys that work on the property, I bought some chain sharpeners from a hardware store. Besides lighting off fireworks, using a chainsaw is pretty high on my list of awesome man-things to do. And when you've got work to do, nothing beats a sharp chain.

1:12pm, Riding in a taxi-van to Otillia's land

After the market I skated down the main street, hitching rides off the back of Motokars part of the way. When I got to the Vegetariano Restaurante, I was right on time to meet Joshua for lunch.

We shared a Motokar from the restaurant to the taxi depot, and by coincidence Otillia got out just behind us. I guessed she came into town to get supplies the same day we did. She organized a car to drive the three of us. I picked up her bag, our driver led us towards the car, and we drove out of Iquitos towards Kilometer 50.

5:53PM - My hammock inside my Tambo

As we neared the sign, the sky darkened and hollered a thunderous roar. The minute we pulled over the heavens opened, and the rain poured down in torrents. We were pelted by fat raindrops as we unloaded our bags. As I ran ahead I prayed my computer stayed dry inside Big Red.

More water started dumping out of the sky than I thought was possible. It was like the scene in *Forrest Gump* when Forrest describes being in Vietnam during the monsoon season: "Little bitty stingin' rain and big ol' fat rain. Rain that flew in sideways. And sometimes rain even seemed to come straight up from underneath." I thought about this as I was jogging along the path and it made me laugh.

I slowed to a walk when I got to the clearing and noticed my raincoat had tiny openings which left me exposed. Water slid down my warm chest and back, and steam rose up from my body. My pants were soaked the minute I got out of the taxi and my boots were now heavy with mud, but I'd loved every minute.

Inside Big Red all my clothes and computer stayed dry, which was a big relief. Luckily, I had the foresight to creatively rain-proof my backpack before I left the hostel. I'm grateful I did, otherwise my gear would've gotten soaked.

My third ceremony is tonight. I feel no stress or fear about what will happen, and even the acrid taste from the Ayahuasca doesn't disturb me as much. As for the purging, that's never been something which bothered me. I feel like I'm getting used to this.

There is a small part of me which feels guilty for still smoking weed. I know it is not allowed on the Ayahuasca diet but it's hard to stop. It's the only thing I have not adhered to from the diet. I even stopped masturbating last week.

I haven't told Otillia that I'm still smoking weed because I don't want to disappoint her. I wonder what makes me so anxious and uncomfortable that I need to smoke weed to relax? Why do I always want to take the edge off with a little puff? I'll bring those questions into the ceremony with me tonight.

When I think about the ceremony tonight I'm filled with anticipation. I feel ready for a breakthrough ceremony. One where I'm given more than just the painful healing I've been experiencing so far. Something more positive that I can take away from this all.

Last Friday, Radolpho came back and joined us for a ceremony. He brought a guy with him who is from New Zealand for his first ceremony. His name is Leigh and he's staying with Radolpho at the Rainbow Community. Radolpho also brought his girlfriend Anna, who just arrived from Spain just a few days ago.

They walked past my tambo with all their stuff a few moments ago and stopped to say hello. Now they're dropping off their bags and getting set up in the big house.

I tried to shake Radolpho's hand but he recoiled and then explained he was on a fast where he's not allowed to touch anyone. He's planning to go an entire month without any human contact. It seems weird to me, but who am I to judge?

I can't imagine doing a fast like that. I enjoy human interaction too much to go a month without it. Everything from passionate sex to a formal handshake is tangible contact, and it is all necessary to some degree.

Another reason Radolpho's fast seems weird is because his girlfriend just arrived from Spain. He has been living in the bush and hasn't seen her for months, and now she's here and he can't touch her--not even a hug. I'd have a hard time with that. I have a ton of respect for his dedication...it's too bad he always seem to be playing the part of a martyr.

Leigh seems like one of the happiest people I've ever met. I can barely look at him without laughing at the way his smile's so big and goofy. When I met Anna she stepped towards me and looked at the crystal on my necklace, grabbing it between her fingers to look at it

CHAPTER EIGHTEEN

MASTURBATION BREAKDOWN

FRIDAY, NOVEMBER 16
6:23am, the big tambo

Last night I had a hard time sleeping. I crawled out of bed, from under the mosquito net, as soon there was enough daylight to justify getting up. My body hurts. I don't feel like I did yesterday. I feel like shit right now. The pain is like the pain I had last week and my joints ache as well.

The pain could be from the addition of the jungle plant medicines to my body, but that feels like a false assumption. It's possible this is my body going through sugar withdrawal. Who knows, but in my regular life I consume way too much sugar. Maybe this is the price I have to pay.

Enough time's passed since I started the Ayahuasca diet for my body to feel much cleaner. It's been long enough it must be detoxifying even my deepest subcutaneous cells. The withdrawal from sugar and preservatives, could be part of why I'm so sore, but who knows.

All I know is that I'm in pain, and on top of the pain I had an awful night's sleep. I couldn't get my mind to cross the bridge from wakefulness to sleep, so most of the night I laid ruminating in my dark thoughts. I tried everything I knew to help me relax, but the more time passed, the more I felt drained.

I feel worn out, and I've never felt like this before a ceremony. I don't think I'll take part in tonight's ceremony. I'm just not up to it. Every other time I've looked forward to the ceremony because I knew it was going to be beneficial. But I don't know anymore. I don't have enough strength to do anything. I'm so tired right now, my heart and soul are so tired.

9:37am, my hammock

Misty steam rose from the wet grass in the warm morning sun. Over the last few hours, the density of my thoughts and emotions evaporated in a similar way. I'm still tired from not sleeping well, it wasn't long enough or deep enough sleep, but that's a technical affair. I'll survive.

One of the goals I had when I came here was to say yes to life. With that in mind, I'm thinking about changing my mind and saying yes to participate in tonight's ceremony. Anything which needs recharging won't work if the battery is dead. That logic is simple. My battery is flat but not dead; there is still some charge left in the reserves.

Most of my desires are vicious wants, not necessary needs, and I see this more clearly now. Thousands of years ago one of my favorite philosophers, Epicurus, described pleasures of the mind and body in this way; "Of desires, some are necessary, some natural but not necessary, and some neither necessary nor natural but the result of an empty opinion. The desire for food and drink and for clothing is necessary. The desire for sex is natural but not necessary. But the desire for a certain type of food, or a certain type of clothing, or for sex with a particular partner, that is neither necessary nor natural."

When I've desired to have more than what was necessary, or natural, I was no longer listening to my body, I was enslaved by my mind.

But now my vices seem less intrusive. It's easier to see my desires for what they truly are, and at the same time they don't seem as overpowering. I am still addicted to tobacco and do not use it with the respect it's meant for. Along with tobacco, I also still smoke weed. Weed is the only thing I have consumed that breaks the Ayahuasca diet.

Well, that's not true. It was the only thing…until last night. I went 11 days without an orgasm but that streak ended sometime between midnight and the early hours of the morning.

Surrounded by thunder and lightning, I was trapped in my thoughts and felt as alone as one can feel. Feverish cold-sweats came and went during the night, and I had pain in my back, knees, shoulders, and elbows. My body ached and it was at this point I gave in and let my mind drift away and fantasize.

Of course Kelsey was my muse. Her youth, so desirable, her perfect soft skin against mine. I pulled her close, her flat stomach against mine where it meets her petite hip bones. Her breasts, her nipples, she brushes them against me and I reach around the small of her back to pull her closer. It's her eyes, and the soft eyelashes draped around them, that have always done it to me.

Those eyes, I remember them as well as if I was looking at them now. They can hold you hostage, and they can give you a future. They believe in your dreams, and they're what make me think love might be real.

As I touched myself and thought of her, my fantasy started to become more visceral. I could smell her skin, feel the softness of her lips, taste her nipples which were hard with the touch of my tongue. I felt her heart beating fast, and her breath on my neck. Gasping, shuddering, and then a sharp breath, an exhale, a whimper, a moan, a kiss, her lips against mine, her nails clawing the skin on my tattooed shoulders, her small hands clutching my muscles. She gripped me tightly, trembling as an orgasm rippled through her body when I came inside of her.

The ecstasy only lasted a few moments, as long as it ever lasts, but it had been long enough that it was a complete and total escape. An orgasm always helps my body relax and my mind become peaceful.

So I did it twice.

I might seem like another classic *gringo* who isn't serious about the guidelines of the Ayahuasca diet, but I'm trying my best.

The only truth in life is that which I deem to be true. I alone determine the nature of my human experience, and I alone determine the value of everything I believe. Sometimes hedonism can be a good thing. Sometimes it is possible to have pleasure with no harm to anyone else, and trust me, there is no way to feel depressed in the middle of an orgasm.

6:18pm, my hammock

Before each ceremony, Juliana prepares a plant bath to *cleanse* our energy. It's a normal bathtub which has been sunken into the ground on the grassy hill between my tambo and Otillia's house. After she fills it with fresh water, she adds different plants according to Otillia's directions.

Roses filled the bathtub tonight! I never expected that I'd walk down and find it filled with rose petals. I also never expected that it would be so calming and relaxing.

There was one point when I dozed off and had a rose-petal-inspired nap. The sunlight waned in the early evening, and I enjoyed the way the bath made my senses feel blanketed in something beautiful.

With the thunder and rainstorms, every day or two we have an amazing show. As I walked back up the hill, a storm came in fast. Something I've been thinking about all day is whether I'll take part in the ceremony tonight, or if I'll back out, but I just decided, *Fuck it*, I'm not going to let my negative thoughts control me. I'm going to allow this process to continue as intended. I'm going to do it.

A playlist of my favorite classical music is playing from my speaker. The sounds of Chopin fill the jungle at dusk. Soon it will be dark and I'll walk down to Otillia's for the ceremony. Now that I've changed my perspective, I feel good about my decision. Rather than try to direct my fate, I'm going to let the medicine be my guide and lead me where it wants. I'm here, all I need to do is say yes.

I am optimistic about tonight because I've continued feeling better throughout the day. That's what made me decide to say yes. Last night was a shitty, sweaty, feverish experience and I felt like shit this morning. Maybe it's my organs detoxifying now that they've finally got a break from eating crappy food. It doesn't matter now and there's no way to know why it happened. I feel better now and that's all I care about.

Releasing everything—all the pain I've put myself through in the past, the injuries, the losses in life, the mistakes and ignorance—was an essential part of the healing process. They no longer serve me and I need to face them to overcome them. I thought time itself healed all things, and what happened in the past was behind us, forgotten over time. But nothing is forgotten; it's just hidden in our subconscious. It's one of our survival instincts.

Everyone has experienced something traumatic in their past. They have chosen to face it and be ok with it, ignore it, or with the passage of time their subconscious has buried it. But it's never gone until you overcome it. Deep down, our bodies remember everything. An animal who didn't learn the dangers of fire wouldn't last long and we have defense mechanisms built into us to defend us from our trauma. Even if we aren't aware of them, these defense mechanisms have evolved with us. Hiding painful memories is a valuable trait.

Being scared of our greatness is what causes us to fail more often than a lack of talent. My weakness is self-sabotaging my success. I am scared to let myself be free. All I'm doing is plundering from my treasures—what I really want is to succeed.

CONFLICTION

CHAPTER NINETEEN
I HAVE A DREAM

SATURDAY, NOVEMBER 17
12:55pm, sitting at the bus stop waiting for a bus back to Iquitos

The pain in my back is almost gone but at random times it still bothers me. I wonder if smoking marijuana is the reason it still hurts. Besides pleasuring myself again last night, it's the only part of the diet I haven't followed directly. Perhaps weed is not letting my body detoxify itself.

The question is, why would something that feels so natural be wrong? How can swinging in a hammock, writing, and smoking a joint be a bad thing? Isn't it an herb which naturally grows here in the jungle? Isn't its purpose clear by the use we've found for it?

It feels like the right thing to do, and I'm going with what feels right. Just like when I used an orgasm last night to escape from sleeplessness. From now on, I am going to decide for myself what is right, and place my own values on things instead of following the values of others.

While staying here, I've only eaten the food that I get served from Juliana, under the direction of Otillia (I assume). I've had a few different bags of nuts and two huge bottles of water in my room, but the bugs got into the nuts right away and I let them have the rest.

I'm proud that I've been able to stick to Ayahuasca diet for so many days. I have been eating lots of rice, vegetables, fruits, and grains. Most meals usually have eggs, sometimes fresh fish or chicken. Lots of the food is boiled or steamed, with nothing more than its natural taste inside it. The diet isn't just limiting what food I eat, it is limiting all the crap that comes with food. The main focus is to help the body return to a natural state, which in culinary terms, means NO seasonings and NO spices.

I am noticing my body is beginning to want different things. It feels like my appetite is leading me towards foods with sustenance and nutrition rather than a never-ending, gluttonous hunger directing me when I eat.

If all I did was follow this diet and nothing else, that alone would be a healthy and detoxifying experience. No sugar, no soda, and of course not a single drop of alcohol since the first night I came to Iquitos.

For lack of a better word, I feel *clean*. Maybe I'm a little bit physically weak from lack of activity, but I feel healthy nonetheless. When I return home there will be more food than I need and I can exercise to my heart's content. Gaining a few pounds of muscle won't be hard. The benefit I will have is I will be rebuilding from a fresh foundation, from a new baseline.

Joshua told me my face looked different yesterday. He said the muscles were more relaxed. It was an honest compliment and when I thought about it later, I noticed I had a sense of ease, or lack of tension, in the front of my forehead, right between my eyes. In fact, during the last ceremony I thought I heard something pop, like a flower bulb had opened in that place. Could this have something to do with what I have read about the Pineal gland?

All I remember is that it's located in the geometric centre of the brain and has something to do with dreaming, the time you die, and the chemical DMT (which is found in ayahuasca).

Perhaps there are parts of my subconscious being healed that I am not aware of. Maybe this calmness has come from having muscles relax I didn't even know were tense. Is the Ayahuasca responsible for my tranquil, homeostatic state? Or is it just my perspective? Is my personal growth just another self-fulfilling prophecy?

Man, if there is one emotion I am becoming more familiar with, it's missing Big Tuna! That's what I jokingly call Kelsey, in reference to the time we ran the hill on Big Tuna Rd., near Los Angeles. I have to laugh when I think about the absurdity of it. What a fun time we had, but we sure worked hard that day.

It took close to four hours to run down the winding hills from the peak of the mountain in Topanga Canyon. We jogged all the way to the ocean, ate some lunch, then turned around and ran back the way we came to my friend's house. After taking a shower together, we collapsed in exhaustion.

I wonder if she would enjoy being in the jungle with me? Would she like the self-exploration, the solitary time, the familiar touch of nature, the Amazon completely surrounding her?

I'll call her today. I miss her and we didn't really get to talk last time. She was working a new bartending job she got at a sushi restaurant. She sounded drunk in her texts, and told me to wait for her to call me when she got off.

I waited around the Karma Cafe until she texted me again hours later. She was driving home and couldn't call because she was in a rush. She had to change out of her work clothes and go meet her friends at the local dive bar for happy hour.

Could we talk tomorrow, she asked.

We could try, I replied.

I wish she had told me earlier so I didn't sit around waiting for her to call. I guess the real reason it raises a sense of alarm is because I care about her well-being. I don't want her to get hurt, or get in any trouble. Drinking at work then driving home isn't the smartest idea. I doubt she wants to finish her fifth year in college with a DUI, considering she already lost her license for that once.

I liked it better when we talked and she was studying the other day. When she's filled with that determination she had then, she seems unstoppable. I remember how I was at that age though: I always thought I would be missing something if I wasn't out partying with my friends. All she's gotta do is pass these last few classes and she's done and can go on the vacation her parents bought her.

5:05pm, sitting at the Karma Cafe

Last night's ceremony was strong and there's no way I could say it was easy. Once again, my back was sore, but I guess my body felt better. It was more just the sadness and achy pain that came back.

I was able to let my mind drift away to a peaceful thoughtless place listening to Otillia sing her icaros, or songs. It was a new feeling, being free in my mind like that.

She has written all the beautiful icaros she sings, and while singing, she keeps the rhythm of her song with a leaf-shaker called a chakapa. She holds this in one hand and slaps it repetitively against her upper thigh, changing rhythms for different songs.

She has performed these icaros for so many years it seems as if not only are they born from her, they are an extension, and part of who she is as a healer. I found moments of true peacefulness listening to her, and I also had an experience which must have been a vision.

I will try my best to accurately recount what I saw, or dreamt about, or thought about, or whatever you want to call it. At the time, it felt like I was falling asleep and about to have a dream, yet I was still awake, and I was able to direct my attention at will. However, just like a dream, the specifics of what happened, which made sense at the time, don't make as much sense anymore.

Also like a dream, my memory of what happened is pieced together, and the pieces are foggy. I'm trying to hold onto them, but they are slowly drifting away.

I found myself in what seem like heaven, or someplace like heaven. As soon as I realized that I was somehow in heaven, a beautiful woman presented herself to me. This space-goddess greeted me, welcomed me towards her, and without more than an introduction she asked me to make love to her. She told me that I was the specific man she had been searching to find for centuries. The reason she wanted to me to make love to her was so I could impregnate her, and she could then have my child.

Although I don't believe we technically spoke, she somehow conveyed to me that she had been scouring the universe looking for me, or more to the point, the spirit of me.

It wasn't as easy as just saying yes: I had to weigh this decision against the amount of responsibility that came with it. I wasn't sure if having glorious sex resulting in a child was the right thing, you know, with this angel lady in heaven and whatnot. What was real and what was not became blurred.

Back in reality I knew I was lying down, on the verge of sleep, and drifting into these bizarre thoughts. I was trying to observe them, as opposed to create them, and they just seemed to be happening. In my body, I became physically aroused and had a hard erection. I remember tucking it into the top of my pants.

My body wanted nothing more than to take the space-goddess, but my mind couldn't decide. My head was sober enough to weigh this moral quandary seriously, without rushing to a decision, but I still didn't know what to do.

I knew if it was all fake, an illusion, then none of it would really matter and the pleasure would be temporary, but if she was a true space-goddess I didn't want to disrespect her by saying no. The problem was I had no damn idea how I could raise a child with her. In the end, I made a choice based on what felt right, and it came from the unbroken, and still healing, part of me.

I turned the space-goddess away. She was angelic, but I knew that it was lust that fueled my feelings toward her. And although I did it for my own reasons, I have to say there's a part of me that turned her down because I didn't want to make a mistake on a universal scale. I was quite unsure what could happen, but like I said, it made more sense at the time.

Logically though, and this sounds ridiculous even as I write it, it wouldn't be sensible to focus on raising a baby right now, especially if it was going to be half-god!

I remember asking her who'd be responsible for raising the child and she told me, "the baby will grow up just like his father teaches him." Of course, I look forward to teaching my offspring, that part didn't surprise me, but what stuck out was she used the masculine when she said "his father"—we would have had a son.

9:47pm in my bed at Alfert's Hostel

Joshua and I met Paris earlier today. Our plan is to go to Paris' land tomorrow and stay for the night to have an Ayahuasca ceremony between just the three of us. Her land is 20 minutes down the river by boat and then a short walk through a tiny village. I'm excited for this mini-adventure.

Joshua asked for, and Otillia gave him, enough Ayahuasca for us to have one ceremony. She asked Joshua straight questions to make sure he was ready to lead us through it and he seemed prepared. She said it would be different from when she is there, but I am confident in the quality of the medicine. It's the same, and I assume we'll drink a similar-sized dose. I'm pretty sure I can handle whatever happens.

I had an inspiring conversation with Joshua on our walk out of the jungle. His encouragement led me to make the decision to stop smoking weed tomorrow. Hearing him talk about living free from addictions made me want that for myself. It's something I don't have currently, but it sounds desirable. I'll try my best—that's all I can do.

CHAPTER TWENTY

THE LAND OF PARIS

SUNDAY, NOVEMBER 18
4:04PM, sitting in a rocking chair on the porch of Paris' tambo

Sitting here in the middle of the jungle, I am appreciating how different, yet equally beautiful, Paris's land is from Otillia's. Speaking of different: I admit, today I woke up at 6 AM and smoked a joint. Morning angst I suppose; this failure took place before I'd even had my morning coffee. It was the only joint I've smoked all day, though.

We took a boat from the main dock in Iquitos and I sat in the back with the kid who worked as the deck hand. He was about 10 years old and laughed hysterically when I took photos of him and changed them in the iPhone app to make him look old or fat.

We landed on a river embankment with tall grass and slippery mud edges. The trail we followed went past an abandoned school house and into a small village with maybe 10 or 15 families in it.

Paris was met with all kinds of affection when we walked through the village. She's obviously been here many times winning the hearts of the locals. Past the village, we picked up another trail and made our way into the thick foliage. About halfway along our hike, two children came out to greet us; they were so happy to see Paris.

Now I'm on her property and sitting on the patio of the two-story house. There's about an hour until the sun goes down and I'm watching Joshua and Paris down below, near a small pond. They're crouched next to each other at the end of the short dock that goes into the pond, preparing a plant bath for us to use before the ceremony.

We can't swim in the pond unfortunately. Paris said there are *biting fish* (!). I felt no need to test her words so I came back up to write.

In Belen market this morning, Joshua knew all the plants we needed to buy for the plant bath, and Paris decided what food we needed to get. It seemed like more food than we needed, but she said some of it was for the poor families, like the one the two kids we had just met came from.

I simply followed them around. I liked watching Joshua collect the specific supplies we needed from the Shaman's Alley. It showed how much he'd learned from Otillia.

Here, just like at Otillia's, we are surrounded on all sides by the jungle and nothing more. This jungle is somehow different though; there is something about the plants that makes it seem like I'm in a totally new environment.

It's hard to explain, but even the palm trees are different here. Some have weird spikes, some have foliage a shade of green different from any other I've seen, and the tallest trees extend themselves towards the sun with their branches making a rooftop much higher than Otillia's. Each leaf is as original as a snowflake and it reminds me how vivaciously alive the jungle is.

In the days since I reintroduced Joshua and Paris to each other, they seem to be falling head over heels in love. It's weird because it is obvious yet not a lot has been openly said about it. They aren't physically affectionate, in fact they barely touch each other, but obviously there's something going on. It seems so obvious.

More than a dozen times, Joshua has hinted that they are meant for each other, but always with an obscure analogy or reference. I see the glassy-gaze of new love in his eyes and it makes me a little sick. It seems so naïve. He's like a lost puppy with its tongue out, tail wagging, oblivious to anything but the object of his affection. I'm not so much turned off by Joshua as an individual; I just don't like the *gaga-googoo* fantasy that accompanies this stage of love, and that seems to have completely overtaken him.

I am not sure if Paris is aware how obvious it is; for her part she is playing it much cooler. I can't stand it, though. The tension has become palpable.

It disgusts me because I have been that person. I have been infected by the sickness of love. I know how at times it can be a totally preposterous, ridiculous, and selfish emotion. It leaves the affected without access to the logical parts of their mind, and in turn that becomes the catalyst which causes their future losses.

4:30am, after the ceremony, alone in my sleeping tambo

By the time the three of us had sat down to start the ceremony, it was taking a noticeable amount of my energy to not feel aggression towards Joshua. His gay, subservient love affair, and how it took over what was meant to be a group event, was tormenting me. I wasn't here to serve Paris, and to be honest, I don't think she necessarily wanted to feel like she had servants. Nonetheless, Joshua directed how we proceeded as though it was all about his princess, but without ever directly saying it.

Just like the medicine can be used in *good* ways, there are ways of using the medicines in *bad* ways, with the intention of hurting others. There are even a few witch doctors who allegedly use Ayahuasca to practice a sort of black magic. The most unique vision I had tonight was dark, which is what the shamans call the Bruha energy.

It must have been my attitude, combined with the Ayahuasca, which created the wild vision that came soon after the ceremony began. It happened suddenly, like a TV was turned on in my mind.

I watched it happen before I knew what was happening. I saw myself kick Joshua out of the second story of the tambo. I didn't kick him physically out of the tambo, it was my *energy* or *spirit* that kicked his *energy* or *spirit*, and he flew through the wall and fell to the muddy ground with a reverberating thud.

The moment he hit the ground, I felt an intense energy and strength rush into me. It felt as though I had been given an infinite amount of power. It was totally orgasmic and completely addictive in every way. I could see him hurt on the muddy ground and it left me with a decision to make.

It felt similar to the decision I had to make with the space-goddess, but this time I didn't need much time to think, and trusted my morals. I jumped down and picked the essence of Joshua up off the ground and returned him immediately to his physical body.

The most memorable vision I had, though, was when I saw every friend I've ever had and every person I've ever met. One by one, they were each brought to the forefront of my attention and I would ask my subconscious, or my spirit, or god, or the Ayahuasca, or whoever the hell was answering my questions, "Is it ok to love this person?" I would only ask this one simple question, and for almost every person I was given the answer that yes, it was ok to love them.

How it worked was weird: I would get a flash of someone's face, or their name, or an old memory, and my current self would be the one to ask the question. Instantly, I would receive a *yes* or *no* answer from somewhere that I knew I could trust. I kept going through people in my life like going through a Rolodex.

Something that came unexpectedly was being told *no* for almost every one of my old friends from Canada. I don't really understand why that would be. Neither did the fact that I saw everyone I've ever known, friends and family, but for some reason I didn't see my parents. Again, I have no idea why that would be.

I use the word *vision* to describe what I experienced because that's the term people use when they are referring to their experiences while drinking Ayahuasca. It seems to be the most appropriate word, but it isn't perfect. It is not like I am taken to some other place. All I'm doing is describing the thoughts I had that I can still remember.

Paris had been very far away in some sort of meditation/spirit world. After more than an hour of being still, she sat up, looked over at me and said, "Sean, you will always have a home here and you are always welcome to come back." It couldn't have felt more authentic. There was something in the way she said it that had real truth, and I don't know what compelled her to break her silence to sit up and tell me that, but I felt so cared for, so accepted. It made me feel safe. If I ever find myself in need and have nowhere to go, I'm welcome here.

Joshua came over to both of us at the end of the ceremony and administered a healing technique of his own design. It was quite powerful. He was either channeling some kind of higher intelligence or being extremely perceptive, but something was different in him when he spoke to us. He told me a lot of things about myself that I already knew to be true, but when he told me my core identity is joy, it really stuck with me.

Being joyful is where I'll be most comfortable, he said, and I must strive to remain in that state. I should be forever in a state of joy. This was great advice for a guy like me because the thing about knowing the valleys of pain is you get a lot of time to study the peaks of joy, and joy is an emotion I plan to ascend to.

I will end with a final thought:

There won't really be a god until science can prove it, until then I'll remain an atheist who believes in Nature.

CHAPTER TWENTY-ONE
MORE POWERFUL THAN EVER

MONDAY, NOVEMBER 19
8:07am, laying in bed in a tambo on Paris' land

It's early morning, I'm sitting halfway up in my bed, and I have a pillow bent lengthwise behind my back. Above my head is a white mosquito net spread out around the corners of the bed, and ahead of me is the door to the small tambo I slept in last night. I'm writing in the fresh daylight, and the protection my little fort provides me feels secure.

A lot of things became clear last night about the reason I'm here, and it began to make more sense why the situation with the blossoming romance between Joshua and Paris was bothering me so much.

What I'm beginning to find with Ayahuasca is that when you bring an intention into the ceremony you are usually faced with some sort of paradox which contradicts, but ultimately helps, you as you sort through what you're shown and find the truth behind your intention.

The last two ceremonies I brought the same intention with me, written on a page in my journal. It was beside me in the ceremony on top of the Thai prayer flag:

Show me love

Yesterday I was shown love. It was my interpretation which made it seem awful, but I had been shown love all day whether I chose to see it or not. As I watched the two lovebirds, and how smitten they were with each other, I got angry, but hadn't that been what I had asked for?

I had to face this first stage of love, because even though many parts are unrealistic and distorted, it is this first stage we must all navigate at the beginning of any love. It wasn't love's fault that I didn't like what I saw. The paradox was that I needed to see this part so I could be reminded of my mistakes. By seeing this, it forced me to remember what *I* loved about the idea of love. I'm still processing this.

Last night, as I said, I became acquainted with the Bruha energy. By that I mean I interpreted the moral decisions I had to make as choices which had a dark side to them. It's something I've never experienced when Otillia was there. With her everything seemed so light and easy.

Last night though, I was given the tempting choice to gain unlimited power by taking it away from another. For the brief second, just after I kicked Joshua's energy out of the Tambo, I was overcome with intense ecstasy. I had a full beaming smile, the kind where your cheeks hurt, and I felt invincible. There might as well have been a warm, soft afternoon sun shining on my body I felt so glorious. It was like having a continuous orgasm, yet at the same time I was comfortable and totally relaxed, happy. As close to a state of nirvana as I've ever been.

The action of my leg kicking out, and knocking Joshua to the ground, happened automatically. It was not a conscious decision, I suddenly just kicked him out of the tambo. What I did next was my choice though. I jumped down after him and picked him up. I brought him back to where I was sitting and cradled him, and then placed him back within himself. By doing this I returned to him the energy I had stolen.

Time seemed to pass in a non-existent way and the entire event transpire so quickly Joshua never actually knew anything happened. After I healed and returned his energy, my amount of energy had returned to normal, but I'd felt what it was like to have another person's energy added to my own, and it was powerful.

There was a lesson for me to learn in this and for the first time I saw myself, and the amount of energy I possess, for what it truly is. I didn't need anything more because I'm perfect the way I am.

Kicking Joshua to the ground gave me so much life energy I almost overdosed. It made me realize afterwords that I don't need anybody else's power, especially not it if hurts the person I take it from. I also learned I had an infinite supply within myself, in fact I have such an abundance that I can supply others if they need it.

What this Bruha energy did was present me with a challenge, and after denying its initial offer, I was given another dark choice. I had seen myself for who I truly was, and the life energy I had, and had felt the power of one other person's energy—now I was given the opportunity to kick both Paris and Joshua out of the tambo with it implicitly understood I'd be given both their energy.

The choice I was given next, to take both Joshua and Paris' energy, was something that'd be difficult for anyone to turn down. The offer implied I would receive double the ecstasy, double the power, double everything I'd felt before. Pure hedonism, instant pleasure, the chance to feel better than I'd ever felt before, even better than sex with a space-goddess, but I didn't cave in, I stood true to my morals—even though it wasn't reality, it was my thoughts and dreams—wasn't it?

This is the reason I didn't kick them both out of the tambo when I was offered. There was no reason to take the energy of my good friends. For one, I didn't need it, and for another, I didn't want to gain this unlimited happiness at the expense of their demise. I desire to be good and I feel like my conscious and subconscious mind work more effectively together when I choose to make good choices.

I have a clean soul, I don't want, or need, to hurt anyone else to gain something for myself. It took self discipline but after turning down the offer I was shown more of my true self, and I could feel myself, and how strong and powerful I am on my own. It was very tempting but it seemed like a very dark and ruthless decision to make, and I realized I'll never need anyone else's energy, I already have an infinite supply.

The thing I can't stop thinking about is that I only heard about the Bruha energy for the first time last week. I was walking past a cafe and joined a lady sitting on the patio to smoke a cigarette. We introduced ourselves and she told me about her interest in the darker side of the medicines and how she'd been studying with a Bruha shaman.

The way she smoked and sipped her coffee reminded me of the White Witch from *The Lion the Witch and the Wardrobe*. She told me stories about the people who practiced Bruha medicine. These stories could have been the moment when the Bruha energy came into me. Or it could have simply been the moment of inception for a silly idea.

Some people would say she passed something dark on to me. Others would note that, just like the geometric patterns I saw, we carry into each ceremony a preconditioned notion about what will happen or what we will see. Since I still had my meeting with the Bruha woman fresh in my mind, my dark vision could have been just a fresh memory coming to the surface.

Who knows, maybe it's not having Otillia here to guide us and regulate the ceremony which allowed the dark energy to become a part of my experience. I can see how her icaros keeps the ceremony consistent and peaceful and gives us something positive to connect with.

Another thing that suddenly hit me was how I have attacked and sabotaged my own success. It is an attempt to bring myself down to the standard of today's society. I convince myself I'm not a good person because I'm not like the people around me, but they are not better, I am just different.

The part of me that hurts myself clashes with the part that feels extraordinary, and therefore it makes sense why I often feel anxious, sitting on my hands, not knowing what to do. I'm developing an understanding about why I felt stuck underneath Paris and Joshua's affectionate puppy love.

Before the ceremony, I thought they both were ignorant and lost in their foolish love. I thought they were disillusioned, because in that situation I have been disillusioned, and hopelessly infected by the fever of love.

Many of the things they were seeing in each other were not things based in reality. I was sure as all young lovers do, they had created stories about love, and their lover, and they were using each other to impress their fantasies of the ideal partner. Like one would press a mold into warm wax, most already have the love they want predesigned, and are looking for a soft place to put it.

Plato said, "Vulgar is the lover who loves his beloved for their physical beauty, for this will fade. The noble and the decent love is that for the unchanging soul," and this is how the sickness of love infects its host. I have learned this lesson more than once. I have been the fool, and been played for one, and I no longer want to be one.

The feelings I had before the ceremony made me feel trapped underneath the issues I wanted to face. During the ceremony, though, a miraculous thing happened. I felt like I rose from below them to a place of freedom high above. I realized I don't need to feel anything negative about their situation. I didn't need to let myself be disgusted. In fact, I don't need to have any feelings about it.

Suddenly I was above them, and my problems, and nothing about the issue mattered to me anymore. This was after I'd seen the enormous amount of power I possess and it had made me feel like I don't need to be cowardly, or feel trapped in a situation like that. I should never let myself be brought down to the dreary place where I feel caught underneath my problems. I can be far above it all if I choose to be.

I am a man who comes from the height of our species, and I was given the message that I am an important soul. Inside of me I carry many virtuous gifts. On this earth, and in this body, I am blessed. I've been given more than a person could ever ask for, and it made me feel grateful.

I am grateful for my intellect, my compassion, my athletic ability, the heightened awareness I have of the world around me: for everything I have.

Last night when I realized that I have even more power inside of me than I need, it gave me the ability to rise above all my troubles. Nothing can bother me because I am not low enough to be bothered by it unless I choose to be.

I thought about how this could be applied to most of the things that hurt me in life. I have often felt slightly crushed by my problems, or by other people's struggles. Whether it was the general suffering of the world, or the specific suffering of an individual, I have often felt like I was trapped beneath a heavy weight. These problems were still there, but they were below me now. I acknowledged their existence without giving them any time or value.

1:22pm riding on the boat back to Iquitos

I am sitting in the back of a boat beside Paris and Joshua. We all have our heads turned towards the river, watching as we peacefully putt along it. I am filled with intense and powerful emotions from the ceremony last night. They are positive and reassuring, and I feel like I have a larger flame burning in me—a renewed zest for life.

What a wonderful and amazing ceremony--without a doubt one of the most personally beneficial life experiences I've had. I am grateful I had the chance to learn so much more about myself. I never would have had the opportunity to see myself this clearly if I hadn't put myself here. It is being in a position so separated from my normal life that allows that.

It's not all from the Ayahuasca that's making me think this way. It's just being here, enjoying the adventure I'm on. I now know I don't need to feel stuck below my problems; whether they are mine or someone else's, I can choose to rise above.

I am strong.
I am able.
Like an eagle, I can fly.
I am Uber-Sean

CHAPTER TWENTY-TWO
AMOR FATI

TUESDAY, NOVEMBER 20
9:04am, Alfert's Hostel

I'm sitting in my bed in Alfert's Hostel and watching an ant highway that must be in the middle of rush hour. It's on the wall a few feet from my bed coming out of a crack in the floor. The ants are moving single file in a line towards the window and a steady lane of traffic next to them was coming down from the window.

The ants are quite small, going up and down in a steady stream, and after a moment I notice the weirdest thing. Whenever they pass an ant going the opposite way, they bump their heads together, then quickly continue in the direction they were going until they bump heads with the next ant they pass.

At first I thought they were just coming and going. It wasn't until I took a closer inspection that I saw they're actually following each other. Single file, and the way they bump into one another perhaps they are communicating to each other.

Alfert's Hostel is at the end of the promenade closest to the Belen market. Resting on top of a scrubby hill, it looks over the shanty village of Belen. I like it here. A private room costs as much as a bunk-bed in a dorm costs at the Green Track. It might be a tiny bit run-down, but there is something about closing the door to your own room that's liberating. All is ok within the security of my private room.

I can hear the rain hitting the aluminum panels of the roof and I can see the water pouring off of them about a foot above my open window. The rain is coming down in a steady stream and behind it, the sky is gray.

I've been laying in my bed, part of the time watching ants, the rest of the writing in my journal. I have deep-house music cranked up from my speakers. I love being loud; there's something about loud music which always puts me in a good mood.

This is the email I sent to some of my friends and family to fill them in on my experience:

Greetings friends,

Last night, after my fifth Ayahuasca ceremony and lots of proper dieting and other plant medicines, I had a breakthrough of gigantic proportions. The ceremonies prepared me for what was to come, and now I truly understand myself for the first time in a powerful and helpful way.

Coming here is a must do experience. MUST DO!

I will happily take you guys any time you'd like. I can show you where to go and what needs to be done so that you may also (if you'd like to) have a chance to understand yourself/heal yourself/empower yourself/find new ideas/understand the natural world and the animal world and our world and how they are connected/understand your place in the universe/release fears/cure pain....etc., etc.

The plant medicines of the jungle are truly teachers. They are a natural way to bring us closer to our natural way. There was a lot of shit my body needed to heal that I didn't even know about, stuff from old injuries and such. The medicines worked on my body first, and now it's brought me here.

As humans we don't understand shit. I don't know how the plant medicines work; it may have something to do with the dream state and the subconscious and conscious interaction, but that's a topic you'll have to ask me about in person cause it would take a lot more words to explain here.

But the main point is you find yourself. You don't become something better than you've ever been. There is no grandeur or illusory self, what you find is your real self. The self that makes the right decisions, the self that wants to be healthy, the self that knows how to get to its personal goals in a more direct way. What you lose is your "shadow" self. The self that's created in your mind but isn't real, the self that stays up all night partying when they have to work the next day, the self that stops for fast food when they are 45 minutes from home, the self that isn't really "you" yet still is, because if anyone should know about having a devil on their shoulders and trying hard to make the right choices, it's me. But I'm pretty sure it's the same for all of us; we all are faced with personal challenges. This has been a chance to transform the way the body and mind work together.

Anyway, this is just a sliver of all of the stuff I would love to share with YOU!

Name the time and place and let's go to the Amazon!

Be back soon, mucho amores amigos!

Sean Hayes

Iquitos, Peru

Today will be the day I say goodbye for good to Mary-Jane. I still haven't smoked a joint since yesterday, but I have some left with me and I feel like now is the time to say a proper *adios* to my green friend for good. My mind is resolute—I will smoke this one joint, and when I leave the hostel I'll begin a new chapter and begin my trek back to Otillia's.

Since it's Tuesday, there will be a ceremony at Donna Otillia's. It's impressive how much of herself she gives twice a week to these ceremonies. Every Tuesday and Friday, people come from far away to see her.

On my way to the taxi depot, I'm going to stop and call Kelsey at the Karma Cafe. Joshua and Paris are going to meet me out there and they said they've got a couple of friends who might also be coming, but I want to hear her voice. I'm almost nervous; even though I talked to her a couple days ago, she still makes me feel excited in the way a good girl should make you feel.

We have been seeing each other for months, but I was in denial and scared to open up to her when it first started. I was protecting myself, not allowing myself to feel anything other than the flash fire of my lust.

It was a real mess when I took her out to dinner a few months ago and tried to explain that I didn't want her to like me. What I meant was that I didn't think it would be the best idea for her to get emotionally wrapped up with me. I had meant it in a good way, but what she had heard was *I* didn't want to like her. Needless to say, at that point the date got a little awkward.

It's different now that I've begun to sort out my position on love and affection. I am becoming clearer on my feelings, in a way that I haven't felt since I was much younger. Love is special, sharing yourself with someone is good, and having someone that wants to reciprocate that is hard to find. Whatever I'd been thinking since I got divorced was wrong. Now I realize that I need to be a better lover, and if I heal my heart, I can move forward.

Last week these romantic, affectionate feelings started to become more apparent. Today I feel like it's important to officially ask her to be my girlfriend. I am ready to have a partner that I respect and I'm respected by. I want to build a relationship with her based on truth and promise, and I want us to both commit to each other. I'm excited to call her and I hope she wants to be with me in the same way.

I also want to tell her that I got the tattoo I told her about two days ago. Next to the stands filled with different artisans, at the opposite end of the promenade from the Belen market, is a man with a tattoo stall. On my right calf, I got script of one of Nietzsche's quote's, immortalizing my feelings. It says *Amor Fati* which translates from

Latin to "love of one's fate." I'll forever love what I'm destined for.

Maybe I can video chat with her and show it to her, that is if the Wi-Fi is fast enough for video. The entire city relies on one satellite for Wi-Fi, and sometimes when it's raining it doesn't work.

I feel encouraged by the path I have chosen to walk in life. I don't have to run from my fate, nor will I ever. I was correct in my gut feeling that I am a good person. I have a lot to offer the world and I'm free to chase after the life I want, hunting for it in the farthest corners of earth. My true strength will always be inside of me. With practice, I'll be able to access it anytime I need.

In the future I will publish books, I will coach champions, I will support my friends, I will be fit and healthy, I will set a good example for others, I will be an honest leader, and I will make my family proud. This is the life I want to live.

CHAPTER TWENTY-THREE

NICK & NICK

WEDNESDAY, NOVEMBER 21
8:10am, my tambo

I want to go into town later so I can call Kelsey. She said yes when I asked her to be my girlfriend and I can't stop thinking about her. Besides that, holy fucking shit! Last night was spectacular, and another formidable ceremony I'll never forget. Soon after I got back to Otillia's, Nick, the long haired kid from Colorado, came walking into the clearing with his dad, Nick Sr.

Nick Sr. had a huge grin and looked happy to be in the jungle. His hair was wet and mostly gray, slicked on his head from walking in the rain.

I could tell it wasn't just being in the Amazon that had him so happy; he was happy here with his son. They seemed excited to be in each other's company. Standing there dripping wet, they finished each other's sentences as they described hiking to the property.

As I might have mentioned, over the last few months Nick Jr. has been immersing himself in the plant medicines of the jungle. He's been doing things like last week when he went to Paris' land solo and did seven days of consecutive Ayahuasca ceremonies. And here I thought I was pushing my boundaries!

Looking at them next to each other, Nick Sr. was like a grown up version of Nick Jr., and they seemed more like old friends than father and son. It made me smile to see them so happy next to each other It was contagious and I felt included in their friendship right away.

When the night came Joshua, Nick Jr., Nick Sr., Otillia and I all drank Ayahuasca together. Paris didn't drink with us because she is on her period. She sat with us but apparently if a woman drinks Ayahuasca during her special time of month, it can bring bad energy into the ceremony.

My guess is it that it probably has to do with how the body manages bodily fluids when you drink Ayahuasca. Almost everyone pukes, and some people have to find a bathroom and take a shit. I have to take a piss at least once during a long ceremony, but blood is something no one wants to see, especially not when they are vulnerable. Keeping a woman away from situations where they might leak blood might be about cleanliness in the physical realm more than anything else.

Our small group made the ceremony intimate and we shared ourselves with freedom. The common thread which wove us together was the inner purpose we each shared, the desire to better ourselves.

We desire the confidence to stand free, apart from the masses. We want to work smarter in life, not harder.

Everyone in the room has in fact already become their own bosses. Joshua teaches, Nick Jr. has something going online, Nick Sr. owns a landscaping company, Otillia is a shaman, Paris was a student and now a property owner, and I coach pro skateboarders.

They are all careers derived from who we are, in whatever form that has become. We have taken control of our lives and want to remove ourselves from the tortures of society in the Western world. We are here to improve ourselves, to break free from what is holding us back. We all want to ascend to the highest peak we can and we are all in it together.

Once we got to the part of the ceremony where somebody starts puking, Otillia started singing her rhythmic icaros to soothe them. It registered in me that it had become easier for me to drink Ayahuasca. That's not to say the taste doesn't get me every time—*bluaaahhk*, it does—but it's less intense now.

It's not just the taste though: it's all a little smoother. My body doesn't hurt as much, I can sit for longer, I have been singing and playing guitar, and I enjoy it. I like being in the moment and making up ad-lib songs. I look outside at nature, or inside at the people I'm with, and I find inspiration in it all. Everyone always claps and thanks me after each song. Even though I know I'm not that great, I know out here I'm one of the best so I am happy it pleases everyone so much.

This ceremony wasn't as profound as the ceremony at Paris', but it was remarkable in other ways. This is what I've come to expect from Ayahuasca. There were no moments of infinite ecstasy, but I did come to the understanding that I have to do more healing while I am here.

12:29pm, riding in a bus back to Iquitos

We are driving slowly in the back of an overcrowded *collectivo*. It was once a mini-van that has had more seats added and is now used as a mini-bus.

Our driver pulled over and packed us in the back, periodically pulling over to pick up more people. Before long the van was filled with locals, babies, chickens, kittens, firewood, and all kinds of things.

Our bags are squished under our feet. I am crammed up against the window next to the two Nicks. It's not as uncomfortable as it sounds, though. It's kind of cozy and the window has a small ledge just big enough for me to fold out my notebook and write on.

During the drive Nick, Sr., has been telling us what an amazing time he had at Otillia's. He said he got a lot from the experience. He'd loved her property and valued the way Otillia guided us through the traditional ceremony.

He told us that at one point he had seen all his old friends, and his family from when he was younger. They had all surrounded him, and after seeing them, and feeling them all, their love was woven into each other and him. Everyone he'd been close to in his entire life was there in his vision.

He tried to explain the support and loving energy he'd felt, but Nick Jr. and I knew it wasn't something that language could describe. He didn't need to explain; we knew what he was talking about. His eyes held the truth, and they didn't deny a word he said.

I'm happy to have met them both. They're inspiring people to be around, but that's no surprise: Colorado seems to make a lot of people like that. Nick Sr. is the type of father I hope to be one day, and Nick Jr. is someone I've looked up to since the moment I first met him at the plaza.

He may be younger than me, but his dedication to living a liberated life is impressive. There's nothing he's scared to explore, nor does there seem to be any fear alive within him. He is a warrior whose war is waged against the conditioned, self-restricted human nature we've all become caged within.

I imagine taking the steps Nick took when he walked off the boat and up the trail that week he brought a week's supply of the strongest Ayahuasca he could find to Paris'. I can hear the random birds and buzzing insects in all their loudness, intensifying the silence of being alone. Sitting there, in the same room I'd sat in with Joshua and Paris, he'd dove head first into his existence as fearlessly as if he was diving from a safe clifftop into the ocean below.

Now that takes balls.

ACTING, NOT REACTING

CHAPTER TWENTY-FOUR

LOST IN RAINBOW COUNTRY

THURSDAY, NOVEMBER 22
6:12pm swinging in my hammock

I feel like I am living in a new world, a world which I'd only touched the edges of before I got here. My existence is blossoming, and I am creating myself anew each day with more confidence in *me*. It gives my life more meaning and I believe in this feeling, I believe in this confidence, and I believe this is how I'm meant to feel.

Like I said when I first came here—*more than love, more than money, give me truth*—and what a wonderful gift the truth has been! The truth that people *do* care, that friends *can* love openly, and *I am* a valuable part of the world.

The confidence and pride I feel about myself is not arrogance. I don't think I'm better than anyone else, I just know that I am a valuable asset to humanity. It is the truth about myself, and nothing more.

I think back to when I first arrived and how much effort it took just to *be myself*. Every day took an enormous amount of effort to get through, just trying to be ok. I learned to ignore the emotional and physical pain I was in each day. When my adventure began I had numbed myself, and was unsure about my place in life. I remember being uncertain if there was any reason to be alive at all.

Now I am certain life has a purpose, if only my own. I understand myself better, and I see opportunities where I can use my gifts to benefit others. I can help people. I will spread my metaphorical lightness, I will use my humor to draw people towards the example I set.

I will be a positive influence on my friends and a confident leader to anyone wishing to be inspired. I will travel as the wind travels and follow its path without resistance. I now see there is a reason for me to be alive, just as much as there is a reason for you to be alive.

After I had lunch with Joshua and Paris, I decided to leave them to their awkward pseudo-romance and hike to the Rainbow Community. The last time Radolpho was here, he gave me directions and invited me to come visit them. Today seemed like the perfect day.

I walked along the trail to the main road with one headphone in my ear. I was listening to a recording of Otillia's icaros that Kari sent me a week before I left.

The reason I'm only using one headphone is because I learned I need to stay aware of my surroundings. I'm not walking along a sidewalk in the city; I'm walking through the jungle. Yesterday I was reminded of the potential for danger walking back.

I was coming back to the property in the evening and felt pretty good. I had successfully made it to town and back, and my headphones were in and the music cranked from the moment I got on the bus.

Hopping and skipping along the jungle trail while listening to my music, I had no doubt I was making good time. I had a small bag on my back and I was wearing my skate shoes, boardshorts and a thin T-shirt.

I was mid-hop from a small stump when out of the corner of my eye I saw a snake. It was sitting exactly where I, in mid-air, had planned to land with my left foot. In the split-second left before I stomped on the snake, who looked as surprised by the immediate threat as I was, I twisted my hips, and spun off-axis towards the right side of my body. My trajectory shifted enough for me to land on my right foot, inches from the snake's head.

Immediately I exploded forward. The snake recoiled into itself, his defense strategy a half-second slower than my retreat. Still spinning to the right, I pushed off and leapt into the air pulling my knees into my chin. I was now facing backwards up the trail.

I saw the snake extending to its full length, its head reaching towards me. There were two tiny fangs sticking out of his head draped by his wrinkled lips that were pulled back. When he was stretched as far as he could, he began to fall towards the earth, but I was still soaring, still spinning through the air. Finishing the perfect 360 degree spin, I landed about 10 feet down the trail. Before I could even think about falling, I was in a top-speed sprint.

In the instant replay in my mind, I can see how close the snake was to sinking his teeth into the exposed skin of my calf. In slow motion, I see his teeth barely miss the skin below my knees that I had tucked as tightly under my chin as I could get them.

Needless to say, it freaked me out and made me want to pay attention to my surroundings better. And that's the reason I only listen to music with one earphone now.

After I reached the shanty homemade bus stop on the main street, I turned right and walked a half-kilometer south. I saw a muddy path on the opposite side of the road. It was wide where it met the asphalt road and narrow further along. I saw where it continued in the distance, and where it crested and descended over rolling green hills.

I crossed to the other side of the road and began to walk along the long, undulating trail. I had been following it for a few miles, slowly steadying my focus on nothing but my footsteps, when I got the feeling someone was following me. There was: it was Raul, the guy I'd met outside my hotel in who'd had a cellphone and helped me call Otillia.

Raul caught up with me and I let him lead the way so I could follow his fast pace along the path. He spoke constantly as we walked, divulging all kinds of information about the jungle. Stopping occasionally, he pointed out anything interesting we happened to pass, and then he'd continue walking while giving me a short explanation.

I learned about a few edible plants and a few dangerous ones, and I also learned the most poisonous snake out here is actually one of the smallest. He showed me one that had been cut in half. We found it by its smell, which he told me is how you know they are close. It smelled like rotten piss, *really* rotten piss.

After we walked for more than an hour, he led me to the shade of a tree and we sat beside a large swampy clearing filled with high grass. We were both drenched in sweat. Raul told me that we should have seen the turnoff for the Rainbow Community by now, but for some reason he hadn't. *We must have missed it*, he said, and I watched drops of sweat fall from my chin and bounce off my knee.

He said he had been planning to go to a different village called the "Fifth Element." It was just as tiny, but it was local people, not like the Rainbow Community. He asked me if I wanted to go with him. Of course I said yes.

A little while later, we turned off the trail and walked down a small path that had plants that seemed even older than most of the plants I've seen. Along the way Raul pointed to a vine that grew surrounding a tree. He knew I would recognize its unique five-starred shape: it was the Ayahuasca vine.

It looked healthy and full and was naturally growing on the side of the path. I pictured Nino going into the jungle and hacking down vines like we did before we chopped them up for the Ayahuasca.

We kept walking along the trail but stopped for a couple minutes when we saw a rapid procession of leaf-cutter ants carrying large pieces of leaves. Soon after, the path opened towards a clearing with small huts. The huts surrounded a fire pit and the dirt was well worn between them. Behind the huts, the jungle encroached on all sides.

Raul was meeting the shaman of the small village to conduct some business. He needed two bags of Chacruna leaf, and he said the shaman at the Fifth Element had very good plants growing on his property.

He pointed towards the shaman once he saw him and we walked together past the fire pit in the center of the huts towards where the shaman was relaxing, asleep in a fisherman's hammock. It was hung diagonally across the small beams supporting the overhang of the roof attached to his hut.

When we greeted him he slowly opened his eyes, rolled his head towards us and gave his eyes time to focus before lifting himself into a sitting position. He seemed happy to see us, and after Raul explained why he'd come, I introduced myself in Spanish. Then, as Raul had suggested before we walked up, I offered him a couple cigarettes as a gift.

The old shaman nodded and smiled a smile that was at least 75 years old. When he reached out to accept my gift, his toothless grin was still able to express his gratitude and his small hand looked like it had been used hard in its lifetime. One of his fingers was crooked with a big faded pink scar and the skin on his arms was very dark with even darker spots scattered along them from where years of exposure to the sun had broken down parts of the epidermis.

He lay back down and lit one of the cigarettes. I didn't have any more American Spirits; I had given him one of the few *Caribe's* that escaped getting wet in my pocket with sweat during the walk. The shaman motioned for me to look at the small shrubs he had growing beside his lopsided bed. His bed was a simple mattress that had been set on top of empty crates, and it looked as weathered as the man himself. The plants were only around two feet high with small tiny branches and small, dark green leaves. In my eyes, it was an unremarkable plant.

The shaman walked over and dug a few of the younger plants up from below their roots and handed them to me. He said something in Spanish to Raul about the plants, who then translated what he said to me. He was offering me a gift to take back to Otillia's land, Raul told me. Without knowing it (or did he somehow know), the gift he offered me couldn't have been better intended.

Last night, Otillia asked me if I wanted to work with Chiri Sonango again today, but I had said no, for now I felt done with Chiri Sonango. I was curious if she had a plant which helped people dream and asked her if there was a *medecina de selva* for that purpose.

I explained that when I sleep it feels like I go from the moment I close my eyes to all of a sudden being awake and it's morning. Sadly, whatever happens while I'm asleep, I don't remember. It's just a dark gray spot in my memory. I want to be able to see, and remember, my dreams.

Sometimes I wake up during the night multiple times, but in the daytime they are faint memories which never stay with me. Besides not dreaming, I am conscious of the fact I wake up during the night, and I can always count on my body to wake me up by sunrise, if not before.

Unfortunately, she told me she didn't know of a plant medicine like that. She either didn't have the plant on her property, or there was no plant like the one I wanted. Either way, yesterday I thought I wasn't going to find a plant meant for what I wanted. But in the middle of the jungle, a different shaman had given me exactly what I was looking for, and from the personal garden next to his bed, no less.

I stood in front of the leather-skinned and soft-eyed shaman. He told me, via Raul, that if I wanted to have vivid dreams, I should place some of the leaves under my pillow when I went to bed at night. Or, if I wanted a more intense experience I should pick some of the leaves, mix them with tobacco and smoke it before I go to bed.

He told a story, translated with extra enthusiasm by Raul, about a man that used these plants to help him find a man that robbed him. The man, who lived on a river, was a fisherman whose canoe had been stolen. He smoked the plant before bed, *and* put the leaves under his pillow. In his dream that night, he saw who the thief was, figuring out where he could find his boat. Who knows if dreams can interact with reality like in that story; all I care about is if it will help me have dreams—any dream will do.

The Fifth Element village was quite interesting. It's so far removed, and yet totally sustained. The jungle provides everything they need. Being there, I didn't feel like I was somewhere remote—when you are surrounded by the dense jungle, it makes you feel like where you are in the center of everything, yet far removed from the center of anything else.

It was an amazing opportunity to see the people living so harmoniously with themselves and nature. They are able to live happily with next to zero commercial supplies. There isn't any way to create any real income all the way out here so they all wear simple clothes, eat food that's foraged or caught, and despite having what we would consider so little, each person looked happy and content.

One of the young boys in the village invited me to his family's hut to have a drink. I was nervous that I was about to drink parasite-infested water when his mom poured me a glass of murky liquid from a pitcher. I took a breath through my nose before taking a sip and realized it smelled sweet. It wasn't water from a sketchy pond like I assumed: it was pineapple juice—thick, pulpy, and fresh as could be. I drank my first cup too fast, but savored my second.

Everyone I met in the village had a relaxed and open expression. The quickness that a smile jumped across their faces showed it was their most practiced emotion. In contrast, it's not something you'll see very often standing in line at Starbucks with a bunch of wealthy people.

Raul explained that he needed to stay a few hours with the shaman and his son so they could pick the fresh Chacruna. I contemplated staying, but thought I should start getting back. I thanked him and said goodbye, and I thanked the shaman for his gift which I had wrapped in a plastic bag, and then I walked back down the path to the main trail.

I found Joshua in his tambo when I got back to Otillia's. I told him about my adventure and meeting the shaman and showed him the gift I'd been given. We went to show the plants to Otillia and she suggested we plant them next to Joshua's tambo so he could tend to them.

After planting the shrubs, I went and rinsed off in the watering hole. After drying off in the afternoon sun, I went back to main house to see Otillia. I walked into the house from the side door that leads to the kitchen and when I entered the living room, there was a couple I hadn't met sitting across from Otillia and speaking English to each other. They introduced themselves to me and explained that they are Indian immigrants who live in Canada. They were very kind, and reminded me of the East Indians I grew up with in Vancouver.

The man was doing his best to explain to Otillia, with Joshua translating, that he was having problems with his family that still lives in India. He was trying to tell her that he worked and lived in Canada, and that his family wanted him to return to India because there were a lot of family problems they wanted him to solve. From his description of his life, it sounded like he lived in continuous turmoil and constant state of panic.

The middle-aged East Indian man and his wife had managed to figure out how to get to Otillia's by the most part on their own, an impressive feat. It showed how serious they were about finding help.

They were seeking guidance from Otillia; a friend had told them about coming here years ago and the man asked if it was possible to have an Ayahuasca ceremony.

Yes, Otillia said, *there would be one tomorrow night.* The man asked, with a desperate look on his face, *can we have a ceremony tonight?* Tonight is Thursday—we normally have ceremonies on Tuesdays and Fridays—but Otillia considered having a special ceremony for the tense man and his wife.

Otillia leaned back in her chair and laughed. Looking over at Joshua and me, she asked if we wanted to have a ceremony tonight. We looked at each other, and I shrugged my shoulders and said, "*Si, gracias.*"

She closed her eyes to ask herself the same question. After a few seconds, she turned to look at the man, whose eyes were pleading, and said *yes, it was possible.*

So tonight, we will have a special ceremony for our new guests. This will be my seventh ceremony, and tomorrow will mark the eighth time I drink the mysterious mixture of leaf and vine.

I feel close to the end of my time using Ayahuasca. It is a much different feeling than a couple weeks ago when I first began this crazy journey, but now my instincts tell me I am close to being finished with what I came here to do.

It feels like I need two or three more ceremonies, and then, for now, will have completed my work with Ayahuasca. I will be ready to return home with a changed and clear perspective on both life and myself. For the time being, I have learned what I needed to learn from the medicine.

I was lost when I first came here, and now I feel closer to finding everything I was missing. It is a calming feeling. The self-exploration process has been intense, but it needed to be so that I could be shown the depths of who I am.

Like drilling into the Earth for precious metals, the layers of dirt and rock on the surface take effort to get through. Once past those layers, though, you uncover the precious metals below. It's good to drill into the essence of your existence, mining your being for the *rarest*, and *deepest*, parts of who you are.

I will have completed my work with Otillia and Ayahuasca when they have completed their work with me. It is coming soon and I am getting more and more excited to go back to the life I left. There's a lot of love and life inside of me, and I want to share it. I'm amazed at how good I feel.

Chapter Twenty-Five
I'M RIDING AN EMOTIONAL ROLLERCOASTER

FRIDAY, NOVEMBER 23
8:00am, my tambo

I woke up intensely sad and filled with pain. Not physical pain but the pain that comes with emotional despair. The only way to describe the intensity and the totality with which it consumes me is like this: imagine your phone rings, you pick it up, and the person on the other side tells you horrible tragic news.

They tell you something severe, like your parents have been killed in a car crash, or they confirm your lover cheated on you, or they tell you there's been an accident and your kids died, etc. Now think of how it feels the instant the bad news ripples through you. Like a violent earthquake, it shakes your very core, and rips apart the foundations of your strongest beliefs.

That is the kind of pain I am trying to describe. The difference is that what I'm experiencing is not a single ripple of bad news. It is painful waves from an unknown storm, crashing over me each time I take a breath.

I feel broken and confused. Why today and why now? I don't want to feel this lonely. Wasn't I just starting to get better?

11:00am, my tambo

The emotional sadness, the dark thoughts, they're killing me today. I don't know why they came back and it confuses me to no end. I thought the overpowering darkness that brews inside of me, occasionally boiling over, was cooling down. If I've been healing the way I thought I was, why did it come back? Have I not taken fuel from the fire, letting the flames burn themselves out?

The pain stings. I was not prepared for it to take over so suddenly; there is no reason for it, nor was there any warning. It hurts like if your hand was being held on top of a red-hot stove. I think that's why people kill themselves. Burning and burning in pain, eventually even the toughest person will cry for relief.

Yesterday, I felt so optimistic and like myself for once. Now, today, I wake up feeling complete desolation and despair, isolated anguish, and a disappointment with my meager existence. It's frustrating. It's not how I want to feel, but it's the way it is.

There's no way to escape it, and on top of that I can't stop thinking about the ceremony I'm supposed to take part in tonight. I'm trying not to attach how I'm currently feeling to the decision of whether or not I'll participate. I don't feel ready for it. I am not ready to be a warrior right now. It is taking all of my strength just to defend myself and there's no way I could fight through it. I'm exhausted, so exhausted.

Part of me feels like it might be an after-effect of the Ayahuasca, but another part of me knows it's much more than that. This suffering I'm going through is something personal. I've been denying it for too long. I need to figure it out once and for all. I can't keep living a life that is so closely attached to so much pain.

Yesterday, Otillia told us sometimes when you have two ceremonies on consecutive nights, the first ceremony will show you something which only makes sense after the second ceremony. Maybe the feelings of pain I'm feeling are the *yin* to tonight's *yang*. Hopefully, if I participate tonight, I'll be given the opposite feelings from what I'm dealing with now. That is seriously the only thing I have to look forward to at the moment.

God, I wish I wasn't taking a break from smoking weed and masturbating. If I could just get a little infinite ecstasy, that'd be great right now. This is exactly the reason I self-medicate with marijuana: it relaxes me, and no pain is strong enough to overpower the euphoria of an orgasm.

Just like every other time I feel like this, I could take the easy route I used to take and get drunk to escape my problems. That never solves anything, though; it just delays the time until you have to face them. In the interim, while you're getting drunk, whatever those problems are seem to find ways to get bigger.

It has taken me too much effort to get here to give in now. Getting drunk is not a real consideration but (forgive me if you disagree), weed is different. It helps ease the pain, and dull the intensity, which right now is razor sharp.

4:33pm, my tambo

It happened again, like every other time so far on this trip. The sadness and pain I woke up with slowly evaporated as the day went on. By lunch time (which would have meant it was time for a meal if we weren't having a ceremony tonight), I'd persuaded myself I had to leave Otillia's immediately. I had given up.

I needed to get out of the jungle and planned to go directly to a hotel with private A/C rooms and regroup. I decided it was too hot here. I was melting, and I'd been in too much pain already today. By lunch time, I had been awake for about six hours, but to me it felt much longer.

There was no way to help myself when my resolution and strength finally broke. Like a robot, I automatically packed my bag for the weekend and walked out of my tambo down the hill. I was done being in the jungle, and I'd succumbed to the convincing arguments my mind had been making.

Before I crossed the clearing, I veered off the trail to Otillia's house and stopped outside. I decided it might be best to tell her I was leaving before I went and disappeared.

I took off my backpack, a lightly packed Big Red, and leaned it against the stairs at the entrance. Calling up into the house, I was answered with a friendly greeting from her bedroom. I stepped up the stairs into the living room and let my eyes adjust to the contrasting darkness.

Joshua was sitting inside in one of the bent rebar rocking chairs, and he looked over at me with a peaceful smile. I sat down in the chair next to him and the plastic straps made a tiny squeal of protest against my weight. They were woven between the rebar frame and had been stretched into a comfortable sitting position from years of use.

I pushed myself backwards and began rocking slowly. Joshua broke our mutual silence by telling me that Otillia would be down in a minute. I was glad he was there because I wanted to speak with Otillia and I needed some help translating. I wasn't sure if I was making an irrational decision by giving up and going into town for a couple days.

Opening the door to her room, Otillia walked gracefully down the steps with short steps. She crossed the room and sat down in the chair across from us.

I started by telling her I needed to take a break from the heat, and then I went on to explain how powerless I felt, how the darkness had taken control of me this morning and broken my spirit. She said she could see I was in pain, but her face told me she was confused as well, but not nearly as confused as I was.

She told me I was very brave to come this far in my healing process, and what I was experiencing now were things I didn't have the strength to face before. This pain now was very old, and therefore it takes more time and energy to heal. But I shouldn't worry, she said, it is ok for me to feel these emotions.

It was reassuring to hear that I was going through a natural part of the healing process. The pain, she reminded me again, comes from letting go of things which I no longer need to hold onto.

I imagine it to be like the pain I've experienced in physical therapy, when I've had to break up scar tissue from an injury. When your body heals from a massive trauma, it hardens into a scar to defend itself, and it leaves the skin fused to the muscles and bones below it.

Sometimes those PT bastards can be real sadists. Attacking an injury in this way hurts incredibly, but it is a necessary part of the rehabilitation process. To aid in the healing process, it is necessary to physically break up the scar tissue by pulling, ripping, and massaging the injured area to regain mobility.

The conscious and subconscious mind, our character and soul, our being and essence, are a much greater part of us than the tiny expanse of flesh we're responsible for. We only have so much area we can injure physically. These larger parts of us are vast, and an injury can leave scar tissue that binds the mobility of our spirit. In contrast, these infinite parts of us have infinite places to be injured and, even more than our body, this is where we are hurt.

Just like in a physical injury, the scar tissue which forms on an injured soul, no matter how long ago, becomes fused and hardened to the soft parts it is surrounded by.

Otillia gave me sound advice and it helped me to step away from the anxious pressure that I'd been trapped under. This gave me some clarity. I was left feeling a little less confused about everything, and with her recommendation I made the decision to stay and participate in the ceremony. Hopefully it's the right decision and gives me what I'm looking for, which at this point is just a tiny bit of happiness.

She put my whole experience into perspective when she reminded me how low my energy had been when I first got here. Compared to what she saw inside of me lately, I had been a shell of myself then and hollow in many places which had begun to be refilled.

Her words were translated by Joshua, and in the process they became even more direct and simplified.

She also told me that I have been reignited once again by the flame of life. She has seen it, others have seen it, and I am a person who's meant to be living with, and overflowing with, joy. It was ironic that she told me the same thing that Joshua had told me when we were at Paris'—I wondered if Joshua talked to her.

Am I learning how to be that person that is filled with joy? I wondered. At that moment I sure didn't feel joyous, but I trusted her when she told me I would feel better soon.

The only thing I still didn't understand is *why now? Why did I wake up feeling so shitty this morning, when I went to bed last night feeling so well?* Whatever it was, the decision to stay helped me feel more confident in being here to begin with. Most people would have quit a long time ago, but I didn't, and I won't. She was right, the fire has been reignited, and if there's one thing I know it's winners never quit, and quitters never win.

I hiked back up the hill to my tambo, unpacked my bags, and stretched out in my hammock, closing my eyes when I found the position I wanted. I tried to ground myself by taking slow, deep breaths. I must have been lying there for some time because the next thing I knew I was about to doze off and I heard Joshua call my name.

He walked up and told me the whole group was going swimming at a place a few kilometers up the road. I decided to join them rather than stay on the property alone. Cooling off in a river sounded like good therapy for me. Besides, it was extraordinarily hot today. The group consisted of me, the Indian couple, Joshua, Paris, Otillia, and Greg.

Greg is the guy that arrived yesterday, right after I returned from the fifth element camp and went to see Joshua. He must have almost caught up to me on the trail—Lisa Hendrick, the sister of my friend Kari, emailed me a couple weeks ago to tell me that her friend Greg was going to be coming to stay with Otillia. He seems like a nice guy, and looks like the strong outdoorsy type, which makes sense since he grew up in the mountains and forests of Montana.

After Joshua and I planted the little bushes yesterday we went and introduced ourselves to him. He taught Joshua and me some yoga moves last night. I was surprised, but by no means disturbed, when he divulged his homosexual disposition.

We all walked out to the road together and when we got there we sat at the broken down bus stop trying to utilize, and share, the shade. Joshua, of course, stood in the bright sun next to the seat he had selected for Paris.

10 or 15 minutes later, a bus pulled over after we flagged it down and we crowded inside. There was a cool breeze from the open doors when we drove off, but it was still hot enough inside for sweat to continue dripping down my back. I felt sorry for the kids that were on the bus with us, their heads level with the midline of sweaty guys like me.

We were on the bus for only a few moments when Otillia told the driver to pull over. We got out of the bus and when it drove off, a cloud of exhaust spat out its tailpipe. Across the street were two roadside restaurants that had smoke coming off charcoal grills.

The smoke curled up off their grills and drifted back over the restaurant towards the circular roof from a large bamboo building. We walked through the restaurant towards it. There was a bridge that led to the bamboo structure and we followed Otillia past the meat that was being grilled. It smelled delicious, the seasoning so strong my mouth started watering.

We walked across the planked bridge, down a ramp, across a path, and towards a staircase that went into the bamboo building. Once inside, we continued to cross the large open room and went down the staircase on the other side onto a strip of grass. There was an open area of bright green grass with a path cut through the middle of it and a sand volleyball court to the right.

The path led to a small strip of beach at the edge of the river. The sand was soft, khaki colored, and very finely grained. The beach was a natural feature of the river from where it bends. The water sat still the near the edge, and in the middle it was faster and even more so along the bank on the far side.

Standing in the water, I looked as far as I could around both corners of the river bend, but there was nothing to see except the thick jungle. There were branches, vines, and leaves protruding from the edges reaching over top of each other in an attempt to steal as much sun as they could from their rivals.

It was refreshing to swim in the river, which I was later told was a small tributary to the *Rio Amazonia*. I watched where the water moved faster in the middle of the river and there were small waves formed from the current. They rolled over each other, and themselves, as they were pulled downstream. The water was a rich brown color, and swirls spun past on the surface that looked like whirlpools at the bottom of a drain.

We swam in the shallow part close to shore because none of us knew if it was safe to go further. We were rightfully unsure if we could trust the currents, or if there were animals we should be scared of. I never saw anything, but who knows! There could have been an Anaconda below the surface waiting to grab the next thing it touched.

I waded past Joshua and Paris, who seemed to be engaged in a conversation of great importance, and asked Greg if he wanted to play volleyball with me and the locals. He looked up at the game being played behind us and told me he wasn't very good, but then shrugged his shoulders and said he'd play anyway.

It was such a fun game. We were right next to a river, in the middle of the Amazon, diving and bumping and spiking the ball in a game of beach volleyball. It reminded me how much I like playing sports.

We both walked away from the game smiling and sweating, but he hadn't been lying when he said he wasn't very good. I played half-decently, but it made no difference because we lost anyway.

Somehow we owed the other team five Soles for the game. I found the right change in my pocket and paid for both of us, and then ran down the grassy bank and jumped into the river. I rinsed all the sand and sweat off of me and let the sun wash over me, looking forward to the ceremony.

1:03am, my tambo

The only time I've felt I have no purpose in life was during episodes of depression and unhappiness. This may sound obvious, but when I'm making good choices, I feel happy. When *I make* bad choices, or when *I'm about to make* bad choices, and especially when *I have made* a bad choice, I feel like crap. Although sometimes I feel like shit for no reason, and those are the times I must fight the hardest to make good choices.

I feel like I have started to find there is a purpose to my life, and that purpose is to be happy and spread my happiness to others. I am meant to be some sort of healer, teacher, guide, or whatever name you want to call someone who dedicates themselves to helping others. I want to return to America and be an inspiration to anyone and everyone who needs it—a leader to my peers, and any departure from this path will be a divergence from my purpose.

If I am unable to live in this manner in the States, or Canada, I will return to South America. This is where I feel welcome and accepted, people understand me here and they like me for who I am—It's a feeling that makes me feel like I'm home.

CHAPTER TWENTY-SIX
BACK TWO BACK

SATURDAY, NOVEMBER 24
7:01am, my tambo, lying in bed

During the ceremony last night, I broke through the pain. All the stars were hiding and it was a little eerie when I entered Otillia's house. When the ceremony began, it was very dark outside and thick clouds covered the sky. I walked past the lit candle in the middle of the room in a small metal dish with two pieces of smoldering wood that filled the room with a thin layer of smoke.

The wood is called Palo Santo, and Joshua told me it's burned for both its smell (like you would burn incense), and also to spiritually cleanse the energy of the room—I presumed we were using it for the latter.

When I settled in a sitting position, with my Thai flag next to me with my written intention on it, I watched the shadows flickering around the room. They made distorted shapes on the wooden walls, and when someone walked in front of it to take their shot of Ayahuasca, there would be one giant shadow.

We all were sitting with our backs against one of the four walls and Otillia was sitting at the head of the room in her rocking chair. After pouring herself a shot, she closed her eyes and sat silently for a moment. Upon opening her eyes, she stood up and softly walked towards the middle of the room to blow out the candle.

Her large white dress rippled in the light from the candle when she bent over, and the room became instantly silent and very dark when she blew it out. There were no stars, no moon, and even the sounds of the jungle seemed to be muted.

I couldn't see or hear her when she walked back to her chair, but I heard the plastic squeak when she sat down in her rocking chair. The ceremony begun and I sat there in the dark. The only noise I could hear was the occasional sound of someone shifting in their seat.

At the beginning of the ceremony, nobody knows how the Ayahuasca will react, for them or anyone else. Even though I couldn't see anybody else in the dark room, I could sense overtones of apprehension within the group. We were sitting there and waiting for the Ayahuasca to do its magic, wrapped in the darkness of the night.

Before anything happened, enough time had passed for me to enter a state of internal calmness. I had been practicing my breathing techniques, trying to enter calm and meditative states for as long as possible during these ceremonies. I tried to observe, instead of control, my Ayahuasca experiences.

Without warning, an explosion of sound and light shook the entire house. The startling interruption made someone gasp, and I heard a quick squeal from somebody else.

The sky crackled to life. I knew at that moment why long ago people thought thunder was the sound coming from the gods fighting.

When it's that bright, and that loud, and so close it's right on top of you, there's no escaping it. I imagined Zeus hurling thunderbolts towards the Earth.

The small room became lit again and again by blasts of purple light. Thunder exploded at the same instant as the lightning flashed and I knew the storm was right on top of us. It shook the wooden house with every strike towards the Earth and I could feel the sky's energy pouring into the room.

Through the door, I could see the jungle illuminated with each white-hot flash of light. The room was still electrified and loud when the Ayahuasca began to start working. People started to vomit,

Otillia started singing *icaros*, and the sounds became mixed together.

The wind and rain, the violent sound of people purging, the rhythm of the chakapa, the smooth sound of Otillia singing, but none of it compared to the power of the thunder and lightning.

I can't remember exactly how long we sat there, or the specifics of what happened those first few hours. All I know is that I had a great time lying back and watching nature's fireworks.

The storm moved past us, and things began to calm down. The sky cleared and the stars came out, sending slices of light between the cracks in the walls. The intense darkness vanished when the moon rose above the canopy of the trees and spilled a yellow swath of light through the open doorway.

I was a little on edge and tried to go back into a meditative state. I drifted away to the harmonic notes of Otillia's voice as she sung her icaros, but I still didn't feel anything from the Ayahuasca.

I sat up to assess myself and my surroundings. I had a bit of pain in my stomach, and as I have done each ceremony, I walked outside to the edge of the clearing to purge. The need to purge usually comes on very fast, and is alleviated soon after I'm done. I came back in feeling much better.

I've come to enjoy the short personal break I take each time I go outside and puke during the ceremony. I never feel rushed and I usually stare up at the beauty of the stars when I'm done, taking a second to wonder at the brilliance of their light.

There were no memorable "visions" during the ceremony, which is weird because it's the same batch of Ayahuasca I had when I did have visions. Sometimes I think I'm having visions and other times I'm not sure. It's strange that I drink the same amount each time, yet it does totally different things.

I sang and played guitar near the end of the ceremony and tried to give some positive energy back to the rest of the group. There are many reasons I am grateful to be here, but the main one is feeling like everyone I've met since I got here truly cares about me. They treat me like an old friend and it makes me appreciate who I am and that I had the courage to come on this adventure.

Today I'm going to head back into Iquitos again. Besides catching up on some website duties, I really want to talk to Kelsey. One of the things I like most about going to town is when I connect my phone to Wi-Fi and all at once, a bunch of sweet messages from her come in. There are many things I want to share with Kelsey; in fact, I want to share everything!

Girls are talented at using language to allure men, and texts can be very subjective, but even though I'm aware of this I can't help but find an enormous amount of pleasure in her messages, and I can't help it that my feelings for her are growing.

I've been thinking about all the times we have been with each other this last year, all the time we've spent talking and relating to each other. I relish those feelings of discovery; it makes me crave her more. I am not sure how I could have been so blind. I really was protecting myself, but this life of mine is too great not to share with someone.

For now, I'm alone in my bed each night and the feeling of being alone is strongest in the morning. I like Kelsey's companionship, and with her I never feel alone, especially not in the mornings. I don't want to let our distance get between us because it feels good to know she cares about me.

On her friend's birthday, it was endearing to see how much effort she put into making the day special. I hope her friends appreciate how much she cares about them.

The last few times I've been back in California, my friends tell me that when they've seen her she talks about me. They say she looks up to me and likes me a ton, and wants to be in a relationship with me. It's a pretty great thing to come back to that.

She knows all about my ex-wife, who technically I'm still married to. Until my-ex wife gets a new visa divorcing her means she'll get deported. Kelsey has never had a problem with it, probably because she can tell I am totally over her. But still, I've been a fool most of the time I've been seeing Kelsey and I know this.

It was foolish to put up so many boundaries between us. The only reason I created them was to protect me from getting hurt. I should have asked Kelsey to be my girlfriend months ago, but I was scared to commit myself to her. I wasted my energy when I tried to make it clear we were just "dating" and not in a "relationship." But that was almost a year ago now, and there's no way to know if she has the same opinion I have now. I want her to be mine.

I am attracted to her independence, and I never want to diminish it. This is why I think it will be helpful if we both take a step back from the party scene. We will get more out of ourselves, and each other, if we do more exploring in nature and traveling more together. We should take more short road trips, do more camping, and sleep in the back of my truck as much as we can.

I've seen it. It's easier for us to be happy when it's just the two of us and we're our true selves—once we stop following the agenda everyone tries to follow back home.

There's a part of me that's always dreamed of having a relationship like the one I want with her now. To find a beautiful, compatible, and loving woman, to create a life together with her, is what I've always wanted.

My cheerful Kelsey is such a beauty, her character so seductive, but is it possible to have this with her? I don't want to force her to become anything she isn't, and I don't want to create a false image of who she is in my mind. It is better if we both remain honest and objective with our feelings.

Being alone in the jungle means I have to accept that how I picture her now, is in part, a fantasy. Even knowing that, I still want to believe we can be a strong couple. However, every strong couple must first have two strong halves, and I am unsure about how strong either of our halves are. It doesn't matter right now, though, because all I can do is work on my half at the moment, and that's what I'm doing.

While I have all these considerations, beneath them I am aware I am falling in love with her, and falling in love with her is making me fall in love with love itself. It is a fantastic emotion. Being here has reminded me how much I enjoy exuberant love affairs. But I must be careful not to embellish the stories in my mind, and I must always stay true to myself.

Over the last year, Kelsey and I have made tons of special memories together. Whether it's camping in the woods, deep-house dance parties at my place, or weekend getaways to Mexico, we've always ended up in each other's arms. She loves to snuggle close to me in bed, and *good lord* do we have incredible sex!

My emotions feel fully alive and it feels great! Yet, at the same time, they feel like simple and pure emotions. It is not an influx of new feelings, or in any way overwhelming or grandiose; they are feelings I've had before. They hadn't left me like I thought. They had been lost, and now they are returning to me.

I have an honest respect for both the *good* and *bad* love can bring, but I am not scared of it. It hasn't all been perfect so far with Kelsey: we've had a couple fights, said shit to each other we didn't mean, emotionally hurting each other for no good reason.

I didn't like when those times occurred, but we're both cut from the same cloth, and we both make mistakes. It takes patience, but I try to remember we both have our own faults. The things which make me feel disrespected shouldn't happen, but it's up to me to stop engaging in that kind of activity.

These are things which now make more sense to me because I don't want to ever fight with her anymore. She can be hard and stubborn, but she's so lovely inside. She was given a tough hand in life with the way her mom left her dad, and I feel sorry she was used as a pawn, and still is, in their divorce. No young girl should have to go through that.

When I look at her when she lets her true self free, I see a little girl, giggling and filled with carefree happiness. I can see it in her eyes. Below the rough, protective layer of her exterior, there's a curious girl who attracts the intrigued boy in me. She is hurt but not broken. She is strong.

Her beauty, her spark for life, and the potential that burns inside of her: these are the things I love most about her, and it's been the adventures and experiences we've shared that have shown me those parts of her.

Now I've healed some of the parts of myself that were broken, I am beginning to feel like it's safe to love again. My love is aflame, which surprises me. I thought for me love was a candle which I'd burned out for good. I didn't think I'd ever feel this way again. Love is a tricky and divine emotion.

There's another reason I'm looking forward to going to Iquitos, and it would be an omission to not mention it. I'm going to find—and smoke—a joint. It has been good to take a break, and I appreciate the intensity of life without it, but I also enjoy the comfort of lying in a bed, relaxing, writing, reading, and smoking a joint.

Maybe I'm kidding myself, but all my instincts are telling me it's ok to smoke a little weed. It was only Sunday/Monday when I last smoked, but I don't feel much different with or without it. Even though I feel quite good at the moment I guess I am a little more anxious. I just want to soothe the parts of my mind that are wound up.

That's my fantasy right now—a good snack, a cold drink, a big joint, and a well-deserved nap on a big bed under a cool, breezy, fan.

1:15pm riding on a bus back to Iquitos

Sitting in the back of a cramped mini-bus is not my favorite way to travel. Just like airplane seats in the economy section, the seats on the mini-bus are too small for me, or rather, I am too big for them.

My legs don't fit when I try to put them straight in front of me because my femur is too long. I have to push my legs to one side and that means my knees are now pinned against the metal side-panel, the bone below my kneecap banging against it each time we go over a pothole.

What should be an hour drive to Iquitos is slowly becoming much longer. Not only is it slow, but it has been stopping at almost every house.

I'm trying to change my outlook and be positive. I am appreciating how agreeable the climate is to me. I can barely recall what it feels like to be cold. All I remember about being cold has been erased by hot nights and even hotter days. It's a distant memory at this point.

I've become aware of something very important during this trip. In relation to where you live, at a certain point it gets so cold that it reaches a point where it starts to physically hurt. The colder it gets from that point, the more painful it becomes.

However, when it's hot, it just becomes more uncomfortable as the temperature increases and the hotter your get. The difference between 95 degree weather and 105 degree weather is just more discomfort, but when it is freezing cold it physically hurts. The difference between freezing and ten below is drastic. I'd rather be uncomfortable than in pain.

When I left Otillia's house today she said one of the kindest things that anyone's ever said to me. She told me I had a lot of courage to come from my country to find her on my own, especially since I didn't understand Spanish very well(or at all). She also said she could see I was becoming happier each day since I got here. It is being reminded of my cumulative improvements that makes any current problems of mine seem less important.

Apparently lots of people come to see her and most of them are scared of what's going to happen. They are afraid of what they will find within themselves—but not me, she said.

I kind of already knew this, but it was confirmed when she told me I've never had the kind of fear that is normal. I was confident, and comfortable every step of the way. While I may not agree it was every step of the way, I do know I have less fear in those parts of my life than other people do.

Also, she reminded me of something she'd told me before: I should never be with someone who doesn't respect me. This is something I am thinking about a lot right now. She finished by giving me her thanks. She was thankful for the opportunity to work together, she finished by saying—all this with Joshua translating.

7:12pm, the Plaza fountain

It's interesting to see the change in my personal view on life since I got here. My perspective has become more truthful. When I analyze myself, the man I see now is much greater than the man I saw before. The strongest emotion I've felt during this trip, besides the charming emotions I have for Kelsey, was the feelings of acceptance when we had the ceremony at Paris'.

That acceptance, and the ability to rise above my problems, were what gave me the confidence to see my true strengths. These are the feelings I always want to stay with me. They are a reminder of how much good my life can offer me. I wasn't given anything new, I have only created a larger expanse within me to explore.

With Ayahuasca, I've reached into the void of my nothingness, all the way from the heights of my greatness, down to dark depths of my existence. I have come away from the experiences with a larger awareness of my weaknesses, and their opposing strengths.

It is a rare opportunity to learn I never need to feel oppressed by problems the way I have, that I am stronger than I will ever need to be and can face any challenge. The fact that I am all I need means I can trust I am capable of fulfilling my life's purpose. If it is possible for any man, it is possible for me.

When I first arrived in Lima, and then Iquitos my first night, I was pestered by the voices from my habits and vices. I wasn't expecting them to be as intrusive as they were. Now they are much less bothersome. I still crave coffee, I would love some ice cream, and my ultimate fantasy is an ice cold Coca-Cola in a glass bottle. They have the kind with the real sugar here, not the high-fructose corn-syrup they have back home.

Some of these are physical desires, and some are simply patterns of my behavior. I want to get rid of them both. I am reminding myself that I turn to these vices because I want to make myself happier, but I won't become happier by masking my emotions. It won't be taking in more of something unneeded that makes me happy.

I can't escape my problems with more food, soda, sugar, cigarettes, alcohol, or weed, because the only way to be truly happy is to become free from these attachments. *Remember this, brain, it is a very important lesson.*

The purpose of life is to be joyful, at least for me it is, and when I bring joy to an endeavor it will become en*joy*able. It works well for me because the core of who I am was built with an unlimited amount of joy. Joshua was the one who told me all this, and I believe him.

It's true: I feel most like myself when I am joyful, and I'm filled with joy right now. This is great for the moment, but I know if I want to stay this way I must continue to act diligently. I must remember everything I've learned during this trip. I *do have the power* to be me always and *it's my choice* what becomes of me.

Now, and when I get home, it will be me who makes the decisions that determine who I am. It won't always be easy to make the right choices, but life isn't easy, nor is it meant to be. We create our destiny alone, and I choose to follow a happy fate.

I choose to release the negativity I have inside of me, and I vow to follow nature's example. She will be my guide, my most trustworthy accomplice, and for now the one I trust with my heart and soul.

Only when I am completely balanced will I be free from pain, and only when I am free from pain—and filled with joy—will I be of any help to anyone else.

CHAPTER TWENTY-SEVEN
NOTE TO SELF: MAKE GOALS IN LIFE

SUNDAY, NOVEMBER 25
9:08am, sitting in my room in Alfert's hostel

I feel lost. It might have something to do with the desperate need I'm feeling to move forward in my life. I need to start writing down personal goals for myself so I have daily and long term objectives to work towards.

It isn't as bad as it has been, but I feel stuck. The darkness is seeping through the cracks of my happiness and it feels like it's on its way, coming faster than before.

Chapter Twenty-Eight
NOW I'M HAPPY, NOW I'M SAD

MONDAY, NOVEMBER 26
10:14am, sitting in my room in Alfert's Hostel

There is something about the moment I lock the door and I'm alone in a private hotel room that makes me feel free. I've been thinking about everything I've learned, and been exposed to, on my adventure so far. It's liberating to feel as safe as I do here, sitting on my bed in a thoughtful mood and listening to music. Most importantly, I'm reflecting on everything I've learned about myself.

When we began the ceremony on Friday, I focused on my intention. It was written on a page in my notebook, laid on top of the Thai flag next to me, and in my sharp, messy handwriting, it said:
Give me the power to be me forever
Looking back on it now, I can see my intention was loaded with contradiction and duality.
Most of my time here has been spent healing, and releasing some sort of pain, and I feel lighter now. I have rested a lot, caught up on sleep, and I feel like some of the heaviness has disappeared. That's the reason I had written the intention for Ayahuasca to '*give me the power to be me.*' I wanted to always feel as happy and light as I did then.
I thought that was me, in totality. I had been feeling good, just as

good as I'd felt in the afternoon before the ceremony, and I thought being *me* was what I wanted—wasn't it?

The answer to that question turned out to be more complex than I anticipated. I believed this newfound confidence was the state of joy I had been seeking. But happiness is actually more like a noun; it's a tangible destination we are trying to reach. Being joyful is more like a verb; it describes the action of getting to that destination.

Just as there is no final destination in life, neither is there somewhere you will get to where you are happy forevermore. It is living *with* joy, *active* joy, which is what we want.

As quickly as I gained these feelings of happiness over the past few days, they left me during the ceremony. I became more sad and depressed as it continued and my feelings slid from joy, to indifference, and then on until I was miserable.

Not wanting to disrupt anyone, I sat quietly and hoped the feelings would pass. There was a slow leak somewhere inside of me and I could feel my confidence slowly deflating like air being let out of a balloon. It was amplified by the fact I was getting sad to begin with, and I continued to sink deeper.

Sure, I sang and played guitar, but it was a vicious and wicked cycle, as I was just trying my best to act the same way I normally did. I wanted the ceremony to end as soon as possible so I could go to bed. By that point I had completely lost my inner zest and I felt *plain* again. I was sunken and confused.

Looking back, I think Ayahuasca was giving me what I asked for. The bliss I'd been lucky enough to experience was so complete, I'd forgotten there are parts of me still in pain, drowned by sadness. That is understandable—there are no mountains without valleys.

The power to be *me* requires the strength to face these challenges. The feelings of bliss I want to have consistently were shown to me just so I could remember them. I was shown the polarity of these emotions when I went from joy to pain, and that's why I need to continue healing: so I don't have to keep going back and forth.

What happened as we got close to the end of the ceremony was unbelievable. I was certain my transformation from happy to sad was only occurring inside my mind. I didn't think anyone else could see, or feel, something was wrong, but Otillia could.

In my opinion, I thought I'd been acting the same way I do any other night. Then out of nowhere, Otillia walked straight towards me in the pitch dark and bent down in front of me. She asked me why I was so sad, *"Por que tu es muy triste?"* Her voice was soft and clear.

As I looked up at her I thought, *how did she know?* It was wild; somehow she knew I was sad, which at the time was something I was still trying to understand. She perceived something had changed in me, and suspected I was struggling—and I was.

By the time we closed the ceremony, I was broken. As much as I tried to let her songs and efforts heal me, they didn't work. On Saturday, I woke up feeling much better, but I still had residual sadness and sorrow carried over from the night before.

Just like on many other mornings, there was a loss of purpose which, for no defined reason, suddenly overcame me. It's part of me, this darkness. I thought it was gone, which was the part that upset me the most, but it's not. The fact that it can come back so suddenly is scary.

What is it? Where does it come from? I was certain all the hard work I've done released the parts that were as dark as the ones I had felt then. If that's not what I've been doing, then what the hell have I been fighting for this whole time?

Enough of my whining. The good news is that after the last few days in Iquitos, I'm noticing my moral compass has gained a heightened awareness. My ability to see good and bad, right and wrong, is more defined, and it makes me feel closer to being aligned with my true self. I am still *me,* but the vices, which are not *me,* don't have as much control as they did before.

It's as though the vices were covering the virtuous parts of me. By healing the dark parts, I uncover more of the bright ones. I still have the ability to make bad decisions, but my vision is becoming clearer, and my awareness wider.

It makes the right decisions easier to make. This is good because there are times when making the right choice can be harder than making the wrong one.

I will always be faced with temptation so it's up to me to make the choice to turn away. It has more to do with my values than it does the temptation. What tempts me is always changing in different places and at different times. Do I exhaust myself denying each specific offering of hedonism? Or is it better to focus on the essence of each desire, which is temptation itself?

No matter what I choose it will be right for me at the time. There is no such thing as making a choice we don't think is the right choice at the time. By having a defined direction, concerning my morals, it's easier to determine what is truly good for me.

I know my choices shape who I become, in accordance with what I want to become, and so I want to make the right choices, for *me.* As Sartre would say, by determining who I am, I commit myself to mankind. We all do. No one is born a coward; a man becomes a coward by acting cowardly. Just like no one is born a hero, a hero makes himself a hero by acting heroically. It is the action which determines the character.

If I want to be the most amazing, ecstatic, and blissful version of myself, I must be discerning and accurate in the decisions I make. I must attune my choices to the highest goals I have for my existence, and I must remember this in each moment of my life.

AM I CHANGING?

Chapter Twenty-Nine
VENI, VIDI, VICI

TUESDAY, NOVEMBER 27
10:31am, my room in Alfert's Hostel

I just got back from skating around the city and picking up as much as I could from my list. I got the cash from the ATM, found some water and nuts at the supermarket, and I happened to skate past an old woman selling Santa hats like the one I bought the kids on Paris' land. No wreaths, though, so I'll try to make her one.

I don't have to look in the mirror to know I've lost weight. I can feel my pants are loose on my hips. All my fat, and some muscle, has melted away in the never-ending heat. I'm always sweating, but I don't mind it to be honest. I like being lean.

I still want to be strong, though, so I'm going to design a workout I can do in my room, something well-rounded, with simple strength-building exercises that only use my body weight.

My hotel workout routine:
-5 sun salutations
-25 in/out sit ups
-5 burpies
-25 crunches

-20 pushups
-25 wide leg sit ups
-20 pushups
-25 lat/side situps/each side
-20 pushups
-25 V-up/lift up leg pulse
-20 pushups
-50 V-sit hammer/side to side
-10 push ups
2x 1:30 wall squat

Total time: 30min

While I was working out, I began to think of some personal goals for myself.

Goals:
-Help people
-Organize financial life
-Live naturally
-Finish writing my next book Beyond Ataraxia
-Finish my book of poetry.
-Get a new contract for the summer of 2013 to coach
-Get a new US work visa (my current visa expires in May)
-Exercise daily
-Live sober
-Skateboard more

CHAPTER THIRTY
DESTROY TO REBUILD

WEDNESDAY, NOVEMBER 28
5:23pm, the big tambo up on the hill

I was awakened by the now-familiar and gentle voice of Otillia, greeting me in Spanish. Folding a corner in my book, I put it down and climbed out of my bed to say good morning. The sun had just risen from behind the trees, and Otillia was standing outside my tambo on the trail next to the long grass, steam rising from it.

I looked around and saw the whole property had a layer of the ankle-high mist covering it. I welcomed Otillia inside to sit down. I am starting to get by in Spanish without needing Joshua's help. Half of my communication consists of creative charades, but each day my vocabulary is growing.

Last night we agreed I'd work with a new plant medicine today. She said it would to start to take effect within 15 minutes and would last three to five hours. Joshua was with us at the time but declined to join in when she offered it to him.

He told me he used this medicine the last time he was here, and that it was, like she had said, a very strong medicine. Although he is usually up for these kinds of things, he said he wasn't personally ready for it right now. He needed more time cleansing.

Since I'd been here a little longer than him, apparently I was ready, and since it is the jungle doctor's recommendation, it became solely my decision if it was something I wanted to do. There was no reason to start backing out of things now. *Fuck it. Yes,* I said.

As for the gift from the shaman at the Fifth Element camp, I tried putting it under my pillow, I tried smoking it before bed, but it doesn't seem to do anything. Still no dreams.

I can't remember the exact name of the medicine Otillia brought me, but it sounds like *Waca pirahna* and it's a powerful purgative. She told me it will complete the physical cleansing process that I started when I arrived. Before a person takes it, their body must be prepared for this plant medicine or it won't benefit from its effects. And mine, after everything I've put it through, was ready.

Otillia handed me a small plastic cup that had about an ounce of semi-clear liquid in it. I lifted it to my nose and saw tiny bits of grainy sediment along the bottom, but it had no smell.

In one quick gulp, I slurped down the sticky-sweet liquid. It coated my throat, thicker and more flavorful than I expected. It tasted like honey. Sliding my tongue along the back of my teeth and swallowing again, I tried to get all the syrup down my neck.

She gave me a calm, reassuring smile as if to reassure me that what I was about to go through was ok.

"*Es muy fuerte amigo, muy muy fuerte, bueno suerte,*" she said. Her advice was that this plant medicine was strong and the way she said it sounded haunting.

I handed her the cup and she told me to come find her this afternoon when I was done working with the medicine. *The afternoon is a long way away,* I thought. I had just woken up; it was only eight in the morning.

She turned and walked back down the path to her house. I sat alone on the doorstep of my *tambo* and watched her disappear into the mist from the wet morning grass. Within a few short minutes, I could feel it starting. It began as a slight discomfort in my gut and then quickly became a fiery heat. When I went to stand up, I was hit by an acute stabbing pain in my stomach. I softly lowered myself back down to a sitting position.

The fire that had begun to burn inside of me kept growing and growing and my stomach felt like there was a bonfire inside of it. Something was building at the back of my throat. It gave a feeling I know all too well by now from all the Ayahuasca ceremonies. This wasn't Ayahuasca, but I knew what was coming next—I was going to puke.

I began to take deep, heavy breaths, and stood up in a hunched position. I took a few wobbly steps away from the doorway. The puke was coming. Beads of sweat started to slide down my forehead to the tip of my nose and chin and then drip onto the grass. I only made it a couple steps before I exploded.

A few seconds later, I was bent over at the waist with both hands on my knees. The entire contents of my stomach had been emptied onto the wet grass and the pile was now steaming alongside the wet grass, being warmed up by sun.

I could feel it on my back and it was hot, too hot. I thought that first puke emptied me out but next it turned into a raging, heaving, shaking, sweating, vomiting experience. I was trembling at this point and the pain kept getting stronger, the knot in my stomach reefing tighter and tighter on itself.

Finally, the intensity of the pain lessened and I had a moment of respite. I dropped to my hands and knees and tried to catch my breath. I felt a few ants crawl onto my bare feet and a bug walking from my knee up my thigh and under the leg of my boardshorts. With a shaky hand, I reached under and swatted him away.

Like a dog, I turned to face my little hut and crawled towards it. With all my effort, I pulled myself up the step and inside onto the wooden floor.

Flat on my back on the wooden floorboards I felt the knot in my stomach get even tighter and I tried to puke, but only a tiny bit of foam came out of my mouth and dripped onto the floor.

I don't know how long this lasted. I kept dry heaving and before long, I was surrounded by a pool of sweat. My beard had bits of drool stuck to it and when I tried to spit, I couldn't. The spit hung from my lip until it touched the floorboard, and I had to grab it with my hand to pull it away from my mouth.

I felt hollow inside and out.

Lying there, the only verdict I could come to about how I felt was that I was the most shattered and ruined I'd ever been. The pain came in waves, the contractions rippled through my entire body. I lay curled up, tensely trying to expel anything I could from the depths of my stomach. I was inside the tambo I had been living in for weeks and grown to feel like home inside, but it didn't matter. There wasn't anything left in me, and nothing coming out.

The most violent part ended after what felt like an impossible amount of time. I had nothing left, not physically, mentally, or emotionally. I was wiped out and laying in a puddle of sweat, soaking wet and freezing cold. Every once in a while, I violently heaved and my abs would wince from the animalistic use they had been put through. My body shuddered with fatigue and horrible sounds came from within me.

The sun continued to rise and it kept getting hotter inside the tambo. I was shaking and shivering when the kiwi guy, Leigh, from the Rainbow Community, walked up to see if I was ok. He told me everyone had heard me puking all morning and they were all worried. He said they thought I must have been dying, it sounded so primal.

He asked if there was anything he could do to help. With a small, gravelly voice, I looked up at him and asked if he could bring me some water. I let my head fall back onto the floor and continued to shiver and sweat as he walked away.

He came back and put a bottle in front of my head on the floor. I looked up at him like a wounded dog, too weak to reach my hand out towards the bottle. I asked, "Please, can you just pour it on my head?" I had absolutely no strength; I could barely get myself sitting up.

Leigh bent down onto his knees and raised the bottle, slowly letting the water stream over my head and down my body. I held myself up on two shaky arms, licking the water from my lips as it dripped down my face.

I thought the worst was done with this crazy medicine when all of a sudden, I felt it moving down from my stomach lower in my body towards my digestive tract. It felt warm, and the fiery feeling came back from deep within me. It was the same warm feeling I had in my throat and the top of my stomach, but now it was deeper, and moving into my intestines.

I asked Leigh for help getting up and I stood, wobbly as a newborn. I asked him to help me get to the toilet. He held onto one of my arms and walked me slowly towards the toilet. I wasn't sure I was going there in time. I could feel what was coming next: next was shitting.

Leigh left me when I told him I could take the last few steps on my own. I heard him step out the door, and I stripped my shorts off, sat down heavily on the toilet, and exploded all at once.

I sat there shitting, sometimes puking, and always sweating. My lower half cleaned itself as thoroughly as the upper half had and I was even emptier.

On the toilet, I shit and puked out every ounce I had inside of me. By the end, there were only tiny drops of clear liquid coming out of both ends. Finally, the contractions went away and I fell forwards off the toilet and crawled away to lie down on the floor under the hammock.

My mind had expired long ago and my muscles were shaking slightly. My thoughts were blank and I felt very far away. I lay on the floor in the fetal position for at least an hour, too exhausted to move. When I regained a shred of strength, I walked very slowly to the watering hole and bathed myself.

There was no one around, the others had already eaten lunch, and I could only wave at the group from the Rainbow Community when they walked past me as they were leaving earlier.

After bathing, I walked towards the building with the picnic tables and saw there was a plate of food that had been left for me. I wasn't hungry but I forced myself to have a few bites of vegetables and drink a couple sips of tea. I sat there, staring straight ahead.

When I finished eating, I walked over to see Nino. He was up at the top of the clearing, preparing a new batch of Ayahuasca. By the time I got to where he was working, I was shaky and lightheaded. I didn't have enough energy to help him do anything so I just sat said down and said hello. He glanced at me and kept working. I decided

I'd be better off lying in my hammock, so I said goodbye.

I wandered back to my tambo, grabbed my notebook and pen, and stretched out in my hammock.

The jungle is getting dark and I'm tired. Clean and tired. I finally feel like I could nap—so I will.

Chapter Thirty-One
TO TOWN

THURSDAY, NOVEMBER 29
6:23am, the big tambo

I'm going into town because there are a few important emails I need to send. Being cut off from the internet gives me a little bit of stress. I feel responsible for the website I'm supposed to be running, and being disconnected makes me feel a bit negligent.

Nothing has gone wrong. In fact, compared to the recent past everything is much better: all our customers are happy, and more visitors keep visiting the site—almost 30,000 each day.

The real disruption is that it's the only tie keeping me from fully *disconnecting*. It could be worse, at least it's a responsibility I enjoy, and I'm good at it. Plus, they kind of need me right now. Even if I do have limited access to the internet for a few weeks, someone needs to be the point person. My boss is busy following his own hedonistic desires that don't always include being reliable.

The thing I'm looking forward to the most in town is having a really cold drink, a hedonistic pleasure of my own. If I wasn't still on the Ayahuasca diet, I would have an ice cold Coca-Cola in a glass bottle, or maybe even a cold beer. But that won't be what I get. To satiate my desire, I will get an ice cold acai and banana smoothie, with no sugar.

Last time I called Kelsey, she was lying in bed, just waking up. It was still morning for her, but closer to the afternoon for me. When we spoke, I felt very social and confident in myself, and at the end warm and full.

She spoke to me in a lovely way, and we shared many things with each other in our long conversation. We talked and talked, and most of the things seemed important at the time, but of course don't really matter. But that's how it goes when you're in a conversation with your best friend (or even better your girlfriend): everything seems important at the time. Of course it does.

I know it's a bit ridiculous to hike for 25 minutes through the jungle, wait for a bus to drive an hour to Iquitos, get a Motokar to the plaza, and then walk to the Karma Cafe, all the while hoping that the Wi-Fi will work once I get there. But being ridiculous is fine by me—and I wrote her a poem I want to send.

Kelsey dearest
As I see you,
A beautiful princess
Smart, yet funny too.

A girl filled with smiles
Chasing fun things to do,
These are the traits
I like about you.

So Kelsey finest
Lay here next to me,
Your body's salvation
Your touch sets me free.

All these things
I've come to see clearly,
All add to the reason
I feel so dearly.

Always be you
Stand tall as you grow,
You're amazing as is
But this you must know.

Even better than all the text messages coming in is when I get to hear her soft, girly voice when she leaves me a voice message. I like to listen to them when I'm lying alone in my bed in the jungle.

Like me, she drinks and smokes, and her girly voice is sharp, and a little matured. For me it's all the sexier. Her voice is beautiful when she sings, but she's only been comfortable enough around me to let it happen a few times. At 23 years old, she is still so young and fresh.

She was one of the first girls I met when I first moved to California years ago. Only 18 then, I was 23 and a total mess. It's only now that I realize how much I care about her, and how much she cares for me. We fell out of touch all those years she was away at school but there's a reason we are back together now. That's why I wanted her to be my girlfriend. I miss her smile, I miss her logical and intelligent mind, and *god* I miss her body next to mine.

Chapter Thirty-Two
I FAILED AND FEEL LIKE SHIT

FRIDAY, NOVEMBER 30
5:02pm, laying in my hammock in my tambo

I came back to Otillia's property in the middle of the day feeling like shit. There is only one person to blame: me. I ate a ton of crappy food yesterday. I blew it; I couldn't help myself; I caved in. The incessant nagging of my vices finally got the better of me.

I started by getting the ice cold Coca-Cola I have been fantasizing about. The place where I wanted to get a smoothie was closed, so I went next door because I *needed* a cold drink. The first sign I was making a bad decision should have been that the store only sold Coke in plastic bottles. Everyone knows plastic bottles are inferior to glass, but I already made the decision to drink a Coke and even in a plastic bottle, it was delicious.

The instant I tossed the empty bottle in the trash can I knew that I'd failed myself and the diet. But I figured that once you've failed, there's no harm in failing some more, so I walked over to get a proper meal at the Karma Cafe. When the waitress came over to me, I couldn't order fast enough. I wanted what's been making me salivate every time I saw someone order it: the tuna sandwich, and of course, another Coca-Cola.

I must have looked like I hadn't eaten in a month, and it's true, not like this at least. But I didn't stop there: after lunch I got an ice cream cone and another Coke. This time, I found where they sold it in a glass bottle and I walked back to Alfert's to enjoy some Spanish TV in my room.

It wasn't until I got back and lay down in bed that I started to feel sick. I sat up with a well-known feeling in my gut and walked over to the open window to empty my entire lunch, and even some of my breakfast, onto the hill beneath me. It splashed onto the muddy grass, sounding like someone had tossed out a bucket of water.

It goes without saying, but I'll say it anyway—I must make better choices about what I eat. I won't always be fed the limited diet my body has become accustomed to at Otillia's. There is no one else to blame but myself. Joshua even warned me that I need to remember my body is more sensitive right now. It is as close to being pure as was when I was a young child and I'm not used to eating the kind of crap that I used to eat anymore.

Other than that step back with the food breakdown, life is wonderful right now. My stomach feels a little shitty, but I'm excited about tonight and my final Ayahuasca ceremony.

What a prolific month I've had. Now that my journey is ending, everything I've experienced so far seems tied together.

There is so much rawness inside of me, a newness which is still settling in. I feel free now. I have seen the most painful parts of myself for what they are and I have the strength to face any part of them. Now I know that without any doubts.

For my last ceremony tonight, I'll be happy with whatever outcome I get, but my intention is for peace within. Ayahuasca heals and operates at a level I don't quite comprehend, and I probably never will. I hope this final experience will fill me with strength. That's the best way I could hope to finish this chapter of my life.

2:00am, after the ceremony, writing by headlamp while lying in my hammock

It was exactly what I wanted. I just came from back to my tambo and the ceremony was *excellente*. I'm not tired yet and I wanted to write. I feel inspired. I have come so far from where I started. Laying here I feel like a new man compared to the boy that lay here a month ago.

In the ceremony, the turbulence and pain that had plagued me the first few times was a distant memory. I worried my lapse in the diet was going to mess me up, but it didn't.

In the middle of the ceremony, I was given the chance to ask my true self, or spirit (or whatever you want to call it), the questions I had wanted to ask all along. The answers were all mysterious, but they left me with a lot to think about. Again, I was pointed towards answers held within me rather than given anything new to add to myself.

At a certain point, when it was the time for me to purge, I followed my intuition, which led me outside. I always end up going to the same spot, and I guess it's the place I'm meant to deposit my old filth. In the daytime I have examined the place where I go. It's a little corner of grass down by the edge of the stream, closer to where the trail goes into the jungle.

It looks just as ordinary and unimportant as any other spot during the day, but it's the spot I feel drawn to whenever I need to purge in a ceremony. It's where I've felt I should go to release whatever Ayahuasca wanted me to get rid of.

When I purge, it always feels like my stomach is expelling a sort of darkness or negative energy. Physically, I guess it is, but it feels like it is also a release of anything negative spiritually, or emotionally. Puking feels like whatever is dark is coming out leaving you with a larger expanse inside. I always feel lighter afterwards.

There was a part during tonight's ceremony when I sat up with a huge smile and laughed. It was a deep, comfortable, belly laugh. I felt happy inside. I don't remember what it was that made me laugh, but I know it came from a place of true happiness.

Throughout the ceremony, I tried to recall the vision I had with the space-goddess. I wanted her to give me another chance. I wanted to see her again. I had no luck. I guess I blew my only chance with her, and now I wish I'd taken that chance when it was in front of me.

Real or not, I sure as hell would love having sex with such a desirable creature right now. Even if what she wants is to father a spiritual space-baby—that's something I'm up for at this point.

My senses became noticeably more tuned in after the ceremony started tonight. The world, and nature, that surrounded me felt incredibly accessible. I could measure the smallest breath of wind, gauge the tiniest shift in temperature, categorize each smell of the jungle, and divide each color into millions of gradients. I could see into the dark and pick out the sound of each drop of rain. I was sensing more, and the Ayahuasca was giving me more to sense. Feeling physically clean (aside from my day of sin) made me feel connected to the elements.

I am pure, I am me, and I want to continue this way of life when I return home. I always want to feel like this. Being natural and clean has filled me with the kind of joy I wanted to find.

The funny thing is that it's much simpler than we try to make it. The key parts of happiness consist of, in my opinion:
Healthy food
lots of water
consistent exercise
recovering and relaxing
close friends
laughing a lot (at yourself too!)
mental challenges
spiritually connecting to the world we live in
and above all, the ability to truly analyze yourself.

I think that's pretty much all a person needs to build a healthy and happy life. When I ate to excess yesterday, I felt incredibly sick, and it was feeling like shit that made me realize how pure my body's become, and how good it can feel.

All this hard work hasn't been in vain. I have allowed my body to return to its natural state. My spirit and soul were begging me to let their light shine. I must not allow myself to cave in; I must keep doing my best.

After working with Ayahuasca for a month, my conclusion is less grand than I originally thought it would be. Everything I've learned, or remembered since I got here, I already knew in some way. That is why it feels like it's coming from within me. I say remember because learning requires the addition of new information, but what I have learned is the value of what I already knew.

As far as anything spiritual, I haven't come to believe anything new. I was optimistic when I got here that there might still be a chance god was alive, but he's not and I'm still agnostic. The only thing I believe more in now is that there isn't any higher power. Now I can see the truth of my existence, and comprehend the nature of myself, as man, more clearly.

All the visions I've had, though, have ended up serving me in some way. They were the pieces I was missing as I tried to put together the puzzle of who I am. After seeing my true self, I am able to have more trust in who I am, and what fate has destined for me.

The connection I believe that exists between all plants, animals, people, the sun, moon, earth, wind, water, and everything between, is real. We are a part of one gigantic living organism. My hunch is the immeasurable space between atoms which binds material together, both living and not, is the common thread that connects everything in our universe.

As I was drifting away to Otillia's icaros midway through the ceremony, the French couple across the room wouldn't stop talking to each other. It began to piss me off. It was obnoxious, sloppy, and distasteful French. It seemed like they were getting louder and louder. This was meant to be a time for everyone to be silent, focusing on the icaros, but the damn frogs were ruining it for me.

These were feelings I recognized, though, and I realized it was a test. The incessant chitchat from the French couple was a test of my patience, my acceptance, and my tolerance. The Ayahuasca probably made their voices seem louder and more obnoxious than they actually were, but like I said, I think it was testing my resolve to stay calm when I'm in an antagonizing situation.

Also, just like when I'd had these kind of feelings before, I became aware the agitation itself was what I had to face if I wanted to move past it. It wasn't the French couple—Otillia had already asked them to please stop talking (although they didn't)–it was my perspective.

Tonight, that lesson was much easier to remember. Rather than worry about how annoying they were, I chose to rise above what bothered me and not let their pigeon chatter distract me. They could do as they wanted. I chose not to let them bother me and the minute I did, they stopped talking.

Whatever the French couple's problem was, it was their problem, not mine. When I stopped letting their voices make me feel trapped, I stepped into the freedom it created.

I need to remember I always have this ability to mentally step away from things that disturb me. Overcoming challenges is what makes us feel rewarded. If I change my perspective, nothing will be a problem.

An eagle is never concerned with pigeons, not when he is so high above them, king of his domain.

PREPARE TO BE CIVILIZED

CHAPTER THIRTY-THREE
MY THOUGHTS SO FAR

SATURDAY, DECEMBER 1
4:30pm, the top floor of the big tambo in a hammock

When the sun gets low in the afternoon, the birds start singing different songs than in the morning. There are different types of birds at this time of day too, and the symphony of the jungle celebrates its last hour of light with a final show.

Once the sun has set, and it's fully dusk, the jungle becomes gray. At first it becomes less and less colorful, then at a certain point the color's gone and it's totally black—but in the moments before then, when it's still gray, the sounds seem to stop and the jungle comes as close to being silent as it ever gets. The daytime animals have hidden, the nocturnal animals are waiting, and the nighttime is coming. They wait for its protective blanket of darkness to hide them.

I feel more connected to nature in this moment than I've ever felt. The rise and fall of the sun, the flashes of lightning, the rainstorm which come fast and hard, the heat each day, the plants that nourish me, the Earth below my feet which I feel embraced by—for now I'm alive, and a thriving part of it. I am an animal born from the same Earth I'll return to. This part in the middle is all I've got.

I feel more natural in my body, and I think a large part of that has come from Ayahuasca bridging together the parts of me which were disconnected. It hasn't been an easy process but it has become much easier.

If someone asked me the best frame of mind to be in when you Ayahuasca, my advice would be as follows:

Kneel down and take the cup.

Hold it in front of you and focus.

Give it your full attention and concentrate on your intention.

Don't wait too long.

With your intention in mind, and without thinking too much, forget about the foul taste and with discipline, imagine what you are about to drink is a beautiful part of nature.

As you slug back the thick shot, think about drinking it like you are drinking a liquid sunset. Absorb its gorgeous wonder, and give it the reverence and appreciation that true natural beauty deserves.

Whether it is a sunset entering my eyes, or Ayahuasca entering my soul, these are nature's gifts. A sunset is easy to appreciate; all you have to do is look West. The best sunsets are seen from high mountain peaks, or untouched beaches, but Ayahuasca has one catch —it tastes like shit—so I try to picture it like it's a green smoothie for my soul. Ever had a beet-carrot-ginger-juice? Good for the body, but tastes like shit. Ayahuasca could be compared to the ultimate shot of wheat-grass—it just happens to be disguised as a shot of jungle medicine-slime that tastes like a moldy-sock reduction.

If someone asked me, that's what I'd suggest. It may sound far-fetched, but for me it made the experience more agreeable. And, trust me, anything that makes the taste less intimidating and the shot more bearable to drink is a good thing.

6:30pm, the top floor of the big tambo, waking up from a nap

I just woke up from a nap and can still recall what was happening as I fell asleep. It struck me that it was a similar feeling as when you drink Ayahuasca and I will try to describe it. My memory is a bit soft and blurry, but I am trying to keep it within my grasp.

I got in the hammock I'm in now and almost went straight into a nap when I laid down. I could feel the sleeping hormones washing through my body as I thought about what I'm going to do tomorrow. Right before I drifted off to sleep, there was a short period when my mind was balancing between being awake and entering a dream.

I seemed to slip in and out, from being awake in my hammock to being awake in my dreams. I was going back and forth across the threshold between my conscious mind and the dream world. It's this middle ground which feels similar to the plane of consciousness Ayahuasca takes you to.

This is what makes Ayahuasca special and different from other psychoactive drugs. It doesn't just bend your conscious perception of reality (like most hallucinogens); it opens a part of our personal reality we don't often have access to. It gives us the ability to enter and extend the window of time we experience between waking (conscious) and dream (unconscious) states.

Thinking back to how the nap started, I remember I was thinking about what I was going to do tomorrow when something bizarre interrupted my thoughts. I can't remember exactly what it was, but it was weird—something strange like fishing for baby elephants with Wayne Gretzky.

I would catch myself when something bizarre like this popped into my head and I would realize I was brushing up against the edge of a dream. However, I was able to stay lucid enough to have influence on how the dream would begin. I could interact with it a bit.

I wasn't directing my thoughts like I was when I was thinking about tomorrow. It changed to me being an observer with criticism. My conscious mind not only could observe, but could also interject proactively.

Balancing between my conscious, sober mind, and my sleeping, dreaming mind, I would give my opinion on what had been created by my subconscious mind that was projecting the bizarre parts, the parts that were coming from the unknown in me.

My belief is when we are aware of being in this state—lucid as I have just described—our subconscious expressions are exposed to our conscious mind. It's like a surgeon having the chance to look inside his patient, and the reason it's an effective healing technique is because our subconscious, or dream state, holds hidden answers to what's broken within us. Even if we think we have forgotten, our goal is not to forget but to know and accept.

Entering these subconscious states, while still having access to our conscious mind, gives each one of us the opportunity to be an observer. As an observer we have the chance to affect our internal and external being. By seeing into what is broken in ourselves, we can repair ourselves.

Remember, one of the greatest evolutionary traits we have is our ability to forget traumatic events. We block out the worst of what we experience to make life more tolerable. We couldn't survive without this skill, and the animal in us wants to heal itself, accepting and moving past the pain.

But we are stubborn animals. With our fancy self-awareness it's hard to know what to do, or how we are meant to heal. This is why I am grateful the Earth provided such an abundance of amazing plant medicines. Ayahuasca is one that's unequaled in its ability to teach and heal.

Drinking alcohol could not be compared to dreaming or drinking Ayahuasca. Being drunk makes you lose control, and after your first drink your judgment becomes impaired, which is different than Ayahuasca. With Ayahuasca, the conscious mind always seems available to interject. Most of all, your judgment remains sound. When I take Ayahuasca, I feel more or less like I do now, straight-minded and sober. (Well, at least enough to be aware of what's happening) I never feel like I've lost control to a drug—just a little like I'm waking up from a nap, lying in a hammock in the humid heat of the jungle.

To ignore our ego, which defines and controls us, and admit what we see, I can understand why people are scared to look into themselves. It's scary to pull off the mask we all wear. The mind is a vast place to become lost in, but why be scared of getting lost in your own? Would you rather be scared of yourself, or scared of the world? We must conquer ourselves first if there's any hope of conquering the second.

All the experiences I've had, both in the jungle and with Ayahuasca, have been the most rewarding, helpful, satisfying, clarifying, amazing, personal, necessary, and magnificent experiences of my entire life.

CHAPTER THIRTY-FOUR
ARE WE AT THE END?

SUNDAY, DECEMBER 2
9:40pm, my tambo

My five weeks in Peru are coming to an end. I feel like the adventure I set out to find is completed for now as well. At first I felt like I *needed* an adventure. Now that feeling has changed, and I feel like my time in the jungle has reached its natural conclusion.

In my adult life, I've never spent so much time alone, digging around in my existence, alone, discovering what it truly means to understand my existence. I can't count the hours I spent reading, writing, and laying in my hammock.

I'm ready for bed, trying to absorb as much of my last night in my tambo as possible. I want to take as much of it as I can with me. I want it to stay a part of me. I have packed my bags and I am already overcome with a sense of nostalgia from all the memories I have made in my little wooden hut.

This tambo will be what I miss the most. It witnessed all I went through. Candles were burned, frogs were discovered under towels, nights were filled with sweat and pain, and sometimes joy. There were times of health, times of sickness, moments of despair and others of revival. More than anywhere else, I healed myself within this little tambo—it was home.

Chapter Thirty-Five
IS IT JUST THE BEGINNING?

MONDAY, DECEMBER 3
8:10pm, the Karma cafe

When I left Otillia's this morning, I couldn't help but feel sad knowing this time I wouldn't be coming back. It only hit me when I was giving everyone a goodbye hug: I was saying *adios,* not *hasta luego* like I'd casually used every other time I was walking away from Otillia or Joshua.

Joshua stood with a tear in his eye. He'll miss me I'm sure, and I will miss him. We fostered each other's growth the same way as brothers do growing up. The elder teaches the younger about strength and courage, and when to take chances. In turn, the younger teaches the elder how about patience and empathy and when temperance is needed. The end result is a brotherhood built on respect and love and with it comes mutual growth.

Otillia, who isn't a big hug person, held me, took my hand, and told me it was up to *me* now. She said I was strong again, I was clean again. She grabbed my other hand. Holding both she shook them a little, like a grandmother would, and said I need to remember I am more *sensitive* now. She dropped my hands and gave me a quick hug.

This was really it. That was my final goodbye. Everything I've experienced will become a part of the chapter in my history I just wrote. When we reach the end of one chapter and turn the page it brings us to the start of the next.

I pondered the term *sensitive* she had used as I walked out to the main road for the last time. Halfway down the trail is a mound of soft clay next to a pool of water. Since my first day, every time I have passed it I've bent down and grabbed a tiny chunk to roll between my fingers.

It's a ruddy gold color and I formed the clay into a cube over and over again in my hand as I walked. I couldn't figure it out; the word *sensitive* seemed to have two meanings. I examined it further and wondered—did being *more sensitive* mean I could *sense more things*, with more detail? Or did *more sensitive* mean I was *more vulnerable*, affected by external stimuli *more* easily and without as much defense?

This afternoon when I got to Iquitos, I met up with Oscar and the rest of the group. Pretty much every time I am in town, I hang out with them. The backpackers and tourists bore me instantly. Keeping up with what's going on with Oscar and the boys (in Spanish) is always good fun.

We decided to walk down to Nikiro which is a bar/restaurant overlooking the river a few blocks from the Karma Cafe. It is a low-key place to hang out and they sell joints the same way they sell beer (*and cocaine*, Oscar likes to remind me just in case I ever change my mind). There isn't any Wi-Fi or food, but for what I wanted right then, it was ideal.

The group and I were all friends now and walking with any of them through town was like having personal body guards. None of the sketchier street people would harass me and the cops never gave us a hard time because I was just a skateboarding gringo and they were poor kids from Belen.

They all knew I was leaving and were: A) going to miss me, and B) hopeful I would give them something before I left. When we got to Nikiro I bought three big Pilsens and split them with the boys. They had the best broken seat waiting for me on the patio when I got there and I joined their circle.

Smoking joints and making jokes, our laughter and smoke drifted out over the Amazon River. My diet was done, and I wasn't going to be stupid and get drunk (or buy me and Oscar cocaine) but I felt like out of respect for my friends, I should honor them with a toast.

I poured myself a cup of beer and joined them. My god, that first crisp sip of cold beer was delicious. It was in one of those small plastic cups, the ones that are semi-clear with a rolled over and tiny bit thicker rim, and really thin sides that crinkle and crack when you crush them, the cracks turning white. Even in one of those cups, and barely cold, it was fucking amazing.

The question they all wanted me to answer was if I planned to return. They were hopeful, but doubtful, I would come back. I guess more than once they'd become friends with a *gringo* who promised to come back and never did.

Every once in a while, one of them would plead with me to give them something—anything—as a gift when I left. They asked in friendly, yet desperate way. They didn't want a memento. After all this time they still wanted the same things from me—my money and clothes—and sometimes I forget I might as well be a millionaire in their eyes.

I sorted through my bag and found a pair of jeans to give to Michael, a few T-shirts for Sam and George, and I gave my sunglasses to Oscar's cousin, Coco. I gave them a bunch of stickers, and I let them figure out who wanted to keep my boots—which were great in the mud, they kept water out, they were sturdy, there was just one thing: they were winter boots and lined with fleece and fucking hot as hell in the jungle. Everything else I needed to keep. Except one thing, which for weeks, Oscar had been asking me to give him: my skateboard.

I gave it to him with one condition: he had to promise to never sell it, especially not so he could buy drugs and alcohol. He agreed with this and told me he would learn how to ride it. The look on his face was classic. He couldn't have been more shocked. Of all my material possessions, this was what the group all coveted the most.

The rest of them were as taken aback as Oscar was; they couldn't believe I was really giving it to him. In South America, particularly here in Iquitos, finding a skateboard is not easy. If you can find one, it won't be cheap: it'll be about seven times more expensive. All in all, I would guess that skateboard here is worth around $300-$400 US dollars.

The board I gave him was a Ryan Decenzo pro-model that he had used to compete on when we were in Copenhagen. He'd only used it for a few hours on the day of semi-finals and had given it to me to when he set up a new one. He won qualifying that day and ended up taking second behind Chris Cole in the finals. Now it's Oscar's board. Its value is far greater in his hands than mine, and I'm curious to know what happens next in the board's life.

Back home I'm fortunate enough my career(s) were always involved in skateboarding. It has provided me free skateboards for more than a decade and I can get another one when I get back to California.

He held it awkwardly, as most beginners do, and looked proud he was the one who'd formed the closest friendship with me, and thus been given my board.

"Well, Oscar," I said with a laugh and patted him on the back, "that's what you get for not ripping me off *too* much." He only charged me a little extra than he should have whenever I got him to help me find what I needed around town. For his part, he reached into his backpack and handed me a few pieces of jewelry to give my sisters, an equally valuable gift for me.

Afterwards, when the beers were empty and we had smoked a second big joint, which handily could be put on my tab with the beers, I laid down on my back with Big Red under my head as a pillow. The Mothership was against my side and the cracks between the wooden planks were big enough for a cool breeze to be pushed up from below like an air hockey table and it was relaxing. A wave of peacefulness washed over me and my eyes bore up at the wispy, bleached-white clouds that were high above. The sun dropping to my left and the temperature dropped a little with it. It was no longer *muy calor*; in the late afternoon it was a *perfecto clima*.

Oscar and his friends lulled me into a trance with the music they were playing, and I found myself drifting off into a pleasant and relaxing nap. It was a mixture of George banging a light beat against his chair and Michael strumming the guitar which he always had with him. His guitar only had four strings, and he'd pluck the strings tenderly. It sounded like he was telling an out-of-tune story and it mixed with their even-paced Spanish conversation. It was all light and musical and it made a calm backing track that put me to sleep.

Where else would I feel that comfortable, and safe enough, to just lie down on the patio of a bar and take a nap? There were no questions asked, and no judgments made.

My physical body is not as picky anymore. If my mind and soul are comfy, let me rest. Sure, a bed is ideal, and a hammock is great, but even a wooden floor in a rickety bar will suffice.

I ordered us another round of beers after I woke up. Sipping from the small plastic cup, it became one of those moments when I felt my senses get excited by the diverse combination of environmental stimuli—the people, the culture, the Spanish, the vast physical separation from the rest of the world, the jungle safely cradling the city, the liberating feeling of being myself, the smell of beer and cigarettes and plants and the wood under me, the colors of the setting sun, the feeling of the temperate air, the taste rich with oxygen—I could sense it all at once.

Tonight will be my last night in Iquitos. The jungle seems to make everyone here, myself included, less judgmental, and that's the difference between this and other cities. There is no escaping the fact the jungle surrounds us everywhere, and it's like the ocean in the respect it commands. Also like the ocean, if you grew up nearby, you learned about its power. Since the time you are young, it is natural to become its pupil and know its strength.

Just like the jungle surrounds Otillia's property, it surrounds Iquitos on all sides. You can't help being intrinsically aware of that fact. With that awareness comes the knowledge that we are all closely sharing one common denominator—survival.

It is something a city like Los Angeles has forgotten. Imagine that! It is dawning on me as I am writing that this is what the people where I live in California have forgotten that. There is so much emphasis on contrived success that we've forgotten we are all the same in essence. We all share that same common goal: survival. It lies beneath everything we imagine to be important. Even though Iquitos is a city, the jungle is so close that survival is something we all need to constantly manage. It is so tangible here that is easy to recognize that we all share that among us.

Of course you shouldn't misunderstand what I mean; it isn't like Iquitos is a spiritual breeding ground. It is a city that's home to many special people, people who are intimately connected to nature. But it also has its dark sides to it. There are signs with warnings against illegal child prostitution, there are cops with large firearms that Oscar tells me are corrupt. There are gringos like the fat Texan who come in and rip off the locals, and there are locals who rip off foreigners, there are locals who rip off other locals and like any developing city, there's the government who often times rips off both the locals and the tourists—and the cycle continues.

I don't think I could write about how grateful I am to everyone I've met and be true with my words. It is so much more than words could describe. My words already don't give the justice my adventure deserves. I just hope I've returned as much as every person who's crossed my path has given me. More than any other part, the people are what gave me what I came here to find. They were the ones that pointed the way, and supported me while I found my direction.

This trip has brought a lot of clarity to my life. I haven't had enough time for this clarity to expose everything about myself I will probably see, but the lens of my magnifying glass is cleaner and will make my exploration more focused. I know there are personal issues I still need to work on, but at least I can see those things for what they are now.

I thought the addition of Ayahuasca was going to give me something I didn't have before, and in one way it has. The difference is that I wasn't given anything new. I was given what I already possessed, which was the ability to see myself without all the delusions and narcissism that had control of me before.

As for having something added to me, there was nothing. I am all I have, and I am all there is. If god was out there I would have seen him, but just as I suspected—I am the god I've been looking for all along.

I feel satisfied with what I've accomplished on this trip, and the hard work I did. I'll always do my best and push forward in life. I will be brave, and I'll take the road that's perhaps more risky, but leads to a more brilliant peak. I have always been this way and it's always felt right, but now I know the reason why.

To have savored the taste of true freedom is a treasure most people are too scared to go looking for in life. It made me realize I can fill my life with as much freedom as I want it to have; I just have to choose the *kind* of freedom I want. First though, I had to break free from my broken beliefs.

I will always be me. I will always face the same kind of choices I have always faced. In this degree they are somewhat finite, just different variations of the same thing. The actions I take are up to me, and I am capable of anything. I just need to take the correct steps and I will get where I want to go.

I have an active mind, and on top of everything else I deal with, I know I'll need to tend to it. I am confident in myself and the path I've chosen to walk. I'm not as confused and depressed by the world as I was before. Not to say it all makes sense, but now the difficult parts of my life which seemed impossible before, I can now see for what they are—challenges for me to overcome.

Sure, it's a simple thing to figure out, but implications mean a lot more for me. It makes me think that perhaps the darkness inside of me is not a personal malfunction. It is a message telling me I have challenges I must overcome, and by working harder and changing my behavior I can do that, and I can be happy.

When I think back to before I got here, I felt was helpless. Like I was being crushed on all sides In contrast, now I feel more confident in myself and not only am I stronger, I'm also more resilient.

My mind and soul feel stronger than they have in years. Even if I'm a bit less physically fit, it was these more personal parts of who I am I wanted to improve, and the body is easy to bring back to good health.

Anticipation would be the word I'd use to describe the way I'm feeling right now. I am curious how my transition will go when I get back to America. Have I been away long enough to expose my foolishness and gain a little wisdom? Will it be hard to return to a place I feel is inhabited by millions of lost souls? Is it going to be easy to remain myself and live the way I now know is best for me?

CHAPTER THIRTY-SIX
LAST MOMENTS

TUESDAY, DECEMBER 4
12:58pm, Star Peru flight to Lima, seat 5A

I'm looking down on the *Selva* as I fly over the Amazon, the jungle that has been my home. All I can see is an expanse of green canopy to where it meets the horizon. I don't think I've ever been this sad leaving somewhere. It's not like I'm breaking into tears, but I'm just going to miss it here, a lot.

It feels like coming here was something that was always destined for me. Like I was meant to come and integrate myself with nature in the jungle. Now, I have accomplished that task.

The most encouraging thing I'm taking away from all this is knowing I always have a home here. It has been more powerful than I could have imagined. I know at any time I can come here unannounced and find friends, food, and places to stay. I am welcome here, always.

Gracias para selva
Gracias para todo
Mucho amores
I'm going to miss you.

CHAPTER THIRTY-SEVEN
HOUSTON, I CAN HEAR YOU

WEDNESDAY, DECEMBER 5
Early AM hours, flying from Lima to Los Angeles via Houston, sitting in seat 37F

These last five weeks in the Amazon have made everything about being in a plane seem ridiculous. The air-conditioning, in-flight shopping, flight attendants with masks of make-up and no smiles—it's all so unnecessary.

Besides looking back on everything I've been through on this trip, I am looking forward to spending the next 10 days with Kelsey before I fly home to Canada for Christmas. I'll only get to see her for 10 days because she'll be gone when I get back to California in the beginning of January.

On New Year's Day, she's flying to Bangkok with six of her closest girlfriends. She's asked me to come with her a bunch of times but I've had to say no because the flight is too damn expensive—but after I went online to check-in to my flight today I looked at my account to see how many air miles I had. Since it has been over a month since my flight to Peru and the miles from my trip to South Africa had been added, my total was just over 70,000 miles—which, as it turns out, is the exact same amount needed (plus $150) for a roundtrip ticket from LAX to Phuket, Thailand.

I haven't told her yet, but I decided *Fuck it,* I'm going to go for it. I am going to say yes to life for the right reasons—I booked a ticket for the 15th of January.

That means that in less than a month I'll be packing Big Red and The Mothership and joining her in Thailand. Every time I think of how enthusiastic her response was when I asked her to be my girlfriend—*Yes! Yes! Yes!*—I feel that same nervous/excited feeling I felt the day I landed here.

She says she wants nothing more than to be my girlfriend and go on adventures with me. I want the same and that's what makes me feel like she is going to be as excited as me when I send her a screenshot of my E-ticket the next time I get Wi-Fi.

That is what I want to share with my partner, and just like I thought in the San Diego County courthouse as I stood on the alter with my ex-wife—*This is either the best decision I've had or the worst decision I've made, only time will tell*—I'm going to try it again. I hope following my heart, going backpacking with my lover instead of solo, in a place like Thailand, will be the best decision I've ever made.

When I see her, I'm going to hold her as tight as I can and give her the truest kiss I've ever given anyone. I am going to trust her. If I want to grow I need to stay open and give her my heart. That's what Otillia taught me.

I give my thanks to the jungle for all it gave me, but I won't dare say *adios,* not yet. My last words will be *hasta pronto, mi amigo*—I'll see you soon, my friend.

THE END

*You never know when you might
need a wizard cap*

ABOUT THE AUTHOR

Sean Michael Hayes was born and raised in Vancouver, Canada. In his younger years he was a professional skateboarder and broke lots of bones. This is what brought him to America, the skateboarding not the broken bones, where he now lives in Encinitas, CA.

He likes to head out into the world on solo backpacking adventures, and when he's not coaching younger professionals skateboarders he's doing something like diving with great white sharks in South Africa or living with a shaman in the Peruvian Jungle. In the last 18 months he has traveled to Spain, South Africa, Thailand, Peru, and about a dozen more countries.

This gives him a diverse social and cultural understanding; the foundation for dynamic and thoughtful literature. His experience with travel, elite sports, global marketing, and social media all compliment his transition into the literary world. After a successful kick starter campaign, Sean's soon to be released books are anticipated by thousands of fans

If you want to connect with Sean, send him a message; @canadianhayes on Twitter/Instagram or Facebook. He posts updates of his adventure on Canadianhayes.com, and if you want to join his super-secret-exclusive-book-club you can sign up now.

MY HAMMOCK

MY TAMBO

OSCAR

BELEN VILLAGE

THANKS!

This book may have my name on the cover, but it couldn't have been written wthout the following amazing humans: Otillia, Paris, Nick Sr. and Jr., T.Rob, Natalie, Ulysses, Vanessa, T.Rob, Clarissa, Helen, Ulyssess, Vivian, Jill, Elise, Nikki, Julie, Blair Alley, Gabriel Aragon, Jimmy Astleford, My aunts and uncles, Julie Barton, Bernard Batitang, Spencer Bing, Steve Black, Troy Blackmore, Alicya Blake, Ali Blythe, Made Boards, Dave Boyce, Dean and Cat Bradhsaw, Catherine Bradshaw, Dean Bradshaw, Erik Bragg, Robert Brink, Jake Brown, Amanda Burchfield, Vera Caccioppoli, Fergie Cancade, Josh Carlton, Amy Carr, Behind the Food Carts, Zoey Ryan, Althea Champagnie, Steven Clare, Von coleman, Daniel Colt Collins, My cousins, Ronnie Creager, Michael Cuff, Shaney Jo Darden, Shaney Darden, Doctor Dave, Ryan Decenzo, Amy Delee, Crew Demere, All my friends in San Diego, Sandra Djasran, Leslie Donnelly, Dylan Doubt, RED DRAGONS!, Leon Drake, Joshua Matthew Duncan, Brian Dvorak, Megan Dyck, Nick Dyer, Geoff Eaton, Bret Eayrs, Bill Engleson, Legends of Enlightenment, Natalie Farr, Sierra Fellers, Susan Free, Greg French, Alex Fuller, Ruben Garcia, Diane B. George, Diane George, Steven Grams, My grandparents, Haley Griffiths, Sandro Grison, Marcus Guerrero, Monty Hamilton, Jordan Hanna, Emily Hastie, Mike Hastie, Dori hayes, Megan Hayes, Emily Hayes, Jillian Hayes, Rhea Hayes, Robert Hayes, Rhea and Rod Hayes, Rod Hayes, Robert T. Hayes, Kari Hendrick, Caitanna Hoffart, Jordan Hoffart, Michelle Huang, Neal Ially, Viv Ian, Moses Itkonen, Colin Mckay, Ryan Decenzo, Scott Decenzo, G.W. Jefferies, Sue Jenks, Tom Jones, Josh Kalis, Paul Karta, Jaimeson Keegan, Ben Kelly, Fergie Kincaid, Brandon and Kira, Adrienne LaCava, Maximillian Lamar, Hayley Lawson, Lisa Lewis, Brandon Lomax, Andrew Lovell, Deanna Lucas, Jared Lucas, Rory Macdonald, CherAnn Macuroy, Rosanne Mailman, Jo Malby, Paul Malina, Will Mancini, William Mancini, Michael Mandarano, Danielle Manzon, Mary Marland, Blair Marlin, Steve Matos, Brennan Mcclay, Roger McClay, Tim McGrath, Matthew Meadows, Becky Mendoza, Eric Mercier, Valerie Michaels, Jody Morris, Leiram Nahir, Haley Nelson, Andrew Nero, Katie Nicole, Chris Nieratko, Carl Nordmann, Deville Nunex, Mo O'Connor, Yulin Olliver, Shawna Olsten, Marius Otterstad, Michelle Paitich, Ron Paitich, Corrie Pappas, James Paxton, Lindsay Paxton, Leslie Donnelly, Ted Paxton, Lynn

Perry, Raini Peters, Jeremy Pettit, Sebastien Pinaz, Mike Prangnell, Desmond Price, Silence in the Library Publishing, Perform X, Paula Radell, Dylan Radloff, Rob Randolph, Dersu Rhodes, Mathias Ringstrom, Nicholas Rossis, Foxy Roxy, Zoey Ryan, Patrick S., Sonya Sangster, Misty Sanico, Manny Santiago, Cindy Santini, Todd Schumlick, Kate Scott, Gretchen Sheckler, Ryan Sheckler, Kira Sheppard, Nate Sherwood, Sarah Sibley, Paula Singer, My family, Ashley Smeltzer, Dustin smith, Alesandra Solari, Nancy Spooner, Caleb Stephens, Vanessa Stone, Steve Stratton, Dave Sypniewski, Chet Thomas, Jamie Thomas, Tyler Thomasson, Paolo Tiramani, John Todrick, Natasha Todrick, Rob Turnbull, Beth Vanboxtel, Leah Vlemmiks, Ava Wallace, Circe Wallace & Charlie, Rob Washburn, Audrey Webb, Jeff Weiner, Everyone I have traveled with, Emily Wolzen, Chanelle Sladics, Kjersti Buaas, Jeff Weatherall, Toty, Monica & La Tortuga, Carmillo, Frank!, All my skateboard friends, and anyone I forgot. Mucho Gracias! If you want to sign up to be a beta reader for my new book, click here.

EXCERPT FROM
Sean Michael Hayes
NEW BOOK

I KILLED A BLACK DOG

THE WAIT
ICE QUEEN
WITH LOVE, THE BAR STAFF

THE WAIT

"Excuse me, will this bus ever be coming?" The woman looked back at the man who had just asked the one question she wished he hadn't asked.

"I guess it will get here when it gets here, sir." Her voice was low. She didn't seem interested in starting a conversation with this man. She sat here almost every day wondering the same thing, but it still didn't change the facts.

"I was told I should be here at noon" he looked at the other people standing around the bus terminal with concern on his face, "Is that the correct time?" He asked, while at the same time wondering why they always seemed so laid back.

She turned to him and said, "Sometimes the engine gets too hot coming over the pass. Then they gotta wait until later in the day. When it cools off they can come down without them brakes getting too hot."

"Yes, but will it be much longer? I have a flight to catch."

"I really can't say sir, there's never any way to know." She looked back at him, "You ain't gonna solve nothing trying to figure out the wait."

"Thank you, and I am sorry to bother you, it's just that I have been told my son is sick and I must return home immediately." When he said this his brow furrowed into deep lines and his worry was intense.

"I am sorry sir, things are just very slow here. The bus will come, it always does, but I cannot say when. And I wish your son well; having a sick child is always quite frightening." He looked like he was wishing the bus would come as much as anyone she'd ever seen, she thought.

"Thank you and yes; yes, it is indeed, and I am aware that things are very slow here." His voice wavered slightly, "that's the reason I came here, to be honest."

It was a waste of time to talk to this man and she knew it, but she asked him anyway, "And where are you from sir?" The breeze was pleasant today and strong enough to keep the temperature right on the edge of where she liked it. This man surely was strange to be here at a time like this. She wondered what he would have been like before, when she still had good days.

"He is damned sick," the man said, "it's happened before with him; they say I must come immediately." Preoccupied by the heat, he didn't notice the breeze. It wasn't much, but small gusts blew from the west and tussled the mans loose hair on the man's head.

"The bus will come sir; you mustn't worry, it is just that things are slow here."

"I know" He said, his head hanging even lower, "that's part of the reason I came."

He never expected when he was younger that this is how it would end. Although he knew it wasn't truly the end, he just felt closer to the end now than when he was younger. Now he could hear the sound of the clock, counting the seconds in his race against time.

"He will get better I am sure; the last time they said it might happen again, but I pray he is in good hands. Perhaps Marie-Angel or his sister Olivia have found where they took him. I just need to get on this damned bus."

"I understand sir, but it's hot right now and maybe that bus is waiting till the suns drops down past the other side, then it can come through the pass with no problem; it is an old bus." She shook her head slowly when she said this to him, she was staring straight ahead now looking up the pass. Didn't this man know anything?

She turned back to him one last time; in her mind it all made sense. "It happens mostly after the big rains, when it gets real hot, most times after lunch, but now it should come any time; won't rain for a couple months I guess. You will get to the airport for the night flight; will that work for you? The night flight?"

"Yes, the night flight will be fine, as long as this damn bus ever shows up."

"It'll come like I told ya. Did ya happen to know they used to bet on it?"

"Bet on what?" He raised his head slightly.

"The time the bus was gonna come in."

"Who would bet?"

"We all would, but the men on the platform ran the bets." She nodded towards a few of the guys leaning against the wall who had their shirts up above their bellies to stay cool. He hadn't seen them but she knew they would all try to hire on as a porter when the tourists came in, if there were any left. "Them boys and us would all wager on what time the bus was coming in, but now of course we all stopped."

"What made you stop?" The man picked his nose, the dry air always made his nose itchy. He was sitting with his head raised.

"A lady they all say was a witch cursed the bus one day and it crashed coming down the pass and everyone on it died."

"That is a horrendous tragedy, I am sorry for any losses you had." He looked towards her now.

"Yes, so if you don't mind I hope you can understand why I would not like to talk about what time the bus comes anymore."

"Yes, yes; I am very sorry to bother you, I only worry about my son, they didn't tell me much over the wire."

"The bus will come sir, things are just slow here." She looked away. What a waste of energy to talk to this man, and at a time like this? There was nothing to do but wait.

Day is done, gone the sun.

ICE QUEEN

Her warmth made me uncomfortable
While her coldness hurt
Her touch electrifying
Although I see now,
Her words were dead
Hands always clenched
Mind often drifting
So much confidence
And such low morals
Posture straight,
Like she'd been taught
But her desires remained obscene
Her steps to rise above,
Meant she stepped on those below
The fury rose inside of her
When all restraint would fall.
She could see perfectly well,
Yet was blind and had no vision
The mental attacks, and sickening deeds
The brutal honesty, which exposed my own lies
A forest of hatred
Growing in a desert of love
Her war-filled past
combined with an un-peaceful present,
She was;
Giver of disease,
Vampire of health.

WITH LOVE, THE BAR STAFF

"Can I please get an Aguila?" he said this politely but he knew things were different after last night. She looked up at him from her phone. She was damned pretty he thought, and like so many girls he had known before her, it was her eyes that held the truth and beauty.

Of course things would be different now, they were always different in these kinds of situations and her eyes were sad and maybe a little angry. The beauty was hiding and the truth he had seen last night was being protected.

"Here," she placed the beer bottle in front of him on the warped and worn wooden bar.

"Como estas?" he smiled and tried his best to speak in her native tongue politely.

"Tu es loco!" there it was, the truth and beauty bright in her eyes now.

"No...." He grinned and said sarcastically. "Yo todo normal..." He laughed when he said it because they both knew he wasn't normal and maybe she liked crazy guys so he asked, with a more serious, "Ti gusta loco chicos?"

"No se"

Her eyes flashed away and then she flashed away, spinning on one heel towards the sink behind her. He had seen it in her eyes though, it was quick but she'd been thinking about him too. It made him happy when her eyes softened.

Just then the Australian couple with dreadlocks walked into the bar and came to sit on the stool next to him. "Dos Mojitos, poor fave-vor" said the tanned Australian guy.

Turning to the man at the bar he said, "Oi mate, how ya going?

Ya shoulda seen all these cunts out in the water today. Mate, I tell ya it was outrageous. One of the poms that's staying here, he went and puked right in his mask 5m down and all these fish started coming up and eating it. Mate, I'm telling ya it was the best shit I've seen in a long time."

"It was rank" his girlfriend added, "the guy said he was eating pizza and drinking rum and coke last night, it was mess!" She would have been a lot more attractive without the dreadlocks but her face was beautiful and you could tell she knew it. They both smelled the same, it was a clean smell.

One of the things he loved about this bar his beer was sitting on was how it turned into an ongoing organic art piece as the night continued. The cold glass beer bottles would sweat and water would drip down over the soggy label onto the wooden bar.

It would create circles on the bar that varied in size, depending on how fast you drank your beer. The circles would be a light grayish color on the dark-stained bar. If you sat in the same seat and drank enough beers, over time, they would join together and create circular designs which only make sense at the time, and were always gone in the morning.

The man looked up at her making the drinks. He liked the way the bartender looked from behind. Thinking back to last night he remembered how soft her skin had been and he wanted to touch it again. Those legs, the color of café con leche; her calves ascending toward the back of her thighs and then disappearing into the shadows of her short dress, and her light summer dress which blew flirtatiously in the wind.

She was mulling the mint leaves and lemon syrup and her hair looked pretty, she was freshly showered and wore a tight braid. He hoped when she turned around things would get better but the Australian turned to the man at the bar and said "Oi mate, we saw you and ol' miss here having a toss in the hammock last night! Good on ya, fine piece of tail for a place like this."

"Andy shut up." His girlfriend punched his huge shoulder with her tiny hand. Australians were never conservative when they drink, were they, the man thought. The bartender looked pissed off. "Would you like to pay cash or should I put these on your room?" she asked this as she slammed the drinks down hard, causing one of the mint leaves to fall off the edge of the glass onto the bar.

"Oh you can go ahead and chuck 'em on the room, and don't worry sweet-stuff, your secret's safe with us, I was just taking the piss out of ol' mate here." All the hippies the man at the bar had ever known smelled like patchouli oil and body odor but the two Australians always smelled like the ocean and nature and they never smelled dirty even though they both had dreadlocks.

The bartender didn't look at any of them, she got red in the face and turned around quickly and busied herself by cleaning up after making the drinks. Embarrassed and angry and this damn Australian wasn't helping anybody out, the man at the bar thought, and tried to change the subject by asking for another beer. "Una mas Aguila?"

Pulling open the door of the fridge, frosty air poured out into the warm Caribbean night. She grabbed an icy cold, sweating beer, and placed it in the center of the water circles stamped in the bar in front of him. She did all of this without looking at him but he couldn't stand it.

"Gracias mi amor," He said smoothly and with a confident voice.

Her eyes flicked up and in an instant her truth and beauty were there. Her cheeks were flushed when she looked into his eyes. The thing he never could have known was that she desired him as much, if not more, than he desired her. That was what made her so angry. He was just a boy and she had let herself get too drunk.

"Con mucho gusto," she said with a mix of confidence and humility. His heart melted and he fell in love with her all over again when she said this. It reminded him of the bedroom last night and the thankfulness she had expressed in her soft Spanish voice. He wished he could make her thankful again right now. She was so distant and he wanted to see her truth and beauty.

Their eyes were still locked, like they had been last night, well before at least. Before it all went to hell. It had started when he opened his bedroom door as she walked past it after coming downstairs from the bar. She looked up at him with a look of yearning and then fell into his arms and without a word they had their first kiss. Her tongue and her lips were as soft as anything he had ever touched, but there wasn't time to think about that now.

"How's about some tequila's darlin'?" The Aussi guy said, with so much volume and force they both turned to look at him.

"Do you want the good stuff or the shit?" With her Latin accent it sounded so cute even though she was angry.

"Get us the good stuff and throw it on my tab and you two cunts have one with us, will ya?!"

The bartender shrugged. The man at the bar looked over at him and then back at the bartender and shrugged as well.

"Ok then," she said half cheerfully, it was just business and there was no truth or beauty in her eyes when she lined up the four shots and cut the slices of lime.

So that's what is going on, the man at the bar thought to himself, he had a flash and remembered the prices of the expensive tequila and he thought about how fresh and clean the hippies always were, even with their dreadlocks, and he decided at that moment they weren't real hippies. It was all an act, they were fake-hippies. Fancy Australian fake-hippies.

"Salud" the bartender tipped her head to them and then tipped it backward, downing hers before any of them had picked theirs up.

"Here's to you two lovebirds!" the Aussie guy always seemed to shout when he spoke and he winked at the bartender and raised his glass.

"Andy shut your trap, ya dick!" his girlfriend tried to punch him, but this time he leaned backwards on his stool and her fist swung past his chest and missed him completely. The force of her punch sent her tumbling off her stool and into his lap and her tequila shot spilled onto both of them. Unfazed, the Aussie guy raised his shot glass a little higher and looked at the man at the bar and said with a slightly cocked head, "Cheers mate!" they crunched their glasses and a little spilled out of both.

When the man at the bar tilted his head back the last thing he saw was the big grin of the guy with dreadlocks, his wet shirt, his girlfriend trying to climb back up from his lap, and on the other side of the bar was the furious stare of the bartender. That image of her face confused him, which confused his stomach and in the seconds afterword, he tried to ride the crashing wave of nausea without succumbing to its strength.

"You're a dick, Andy!" his girlfriend leaned over and shouted from the barstool she had returned to.

"Oh, you love me sweetie, you know it..." His grin had the qualities of both puppy and child which made him seem like one of those guys who would be impossible to get angry at.

"You're an asshole; he's an asshole, right?" his girlfriend turned towards the bartender and slumped both elbows down heavily in front of her on the bar. The bartender wasn't going to say anything to confirm her accusations, he was an asshole, but she was an asshole too, they were both assholes and it was her own fault she had fallen out of her chair.

"I'm going to bed Andy, why don't you stay here with the people you LOVE sooooo much. I'll be in bed, you're such a jerk."

"Oh relax will ya? Don't get your titties tied. Sit down, you're all right." She was standing now and had been about to walk away but instead moved closer to him.

"Have another drink; you'll be fine." He reached over and touched her when he said this. Pulling her closer with one hand, he slid a dreadlock behind her ear with his free hand and then leaned forward to kiss her gently on the cheek.

The bartender looked away. Love was weird she thought, it made you do the weirdest things and she turned her head back and forth slowly. His girlfriend reached her tiny hand up into his massive pile of matted hair and pulled the fake-hippie guy toward her so she could whisper something in his ear.

"Well kids, that's it for us!" he shot up straight and quickly finished the last sips of both their drinks. When he stood up from his stool he was surprisingly bigger than his girlfriend. He bent down and grabbed her around the waist and straightened his legs to stand up and when he was standing he swung her around and placed her bent over on his right shoulder.

"The ol' lady told me she wants to watch some porn and get kinky tonight so don't bother coming to find us for a few hours!" He shouted this back towards them and they didn't know it at the time but that was the last words either of them ever heard that fake-hippie guy say.

His girlfriend was still shouting as he carried her across the bar and down the stairs, "You're such an asshole Andy, put me down, I AM NOT having SEX with YOU tonight you pig, and you sure as hell ain't getting kinky, you can't say that type of shit, ANDY, put me down…." But he had already carried her down the stairs and out of the bar and they were gone.

The bartender looked at him, the man at the bar who was really a boy. Alone with him she had no one else to be angry at. She stared her icy stare at him, even though she liked him. She leaned onto the bar and he leaned onto the bar and he smiled even though she didn't. Her hardness softened as she stared at him, and into him, and he realized he was close enough to kiss her if he wanted to, so he did.

"Stop it!" She slapped him and recoiled, "Why the hell did you do that?" When she said this the truth and beauty was there, though now it was a rage of truth and a blaze of beauty and it was all of her. She splashed the ice out of the cups from the finished mojitos and then walked out from behind the bar towards him.

"I'm sorry, I didn't mean anything, I just thought…" His voice trailed off, she looked angry.

"You're a real asshole" she slapped him hard across the face and it stung.

"Tranquilo, princessa." He stood up over her and grabbed both of her wrists before she could slap him again. "It's all good." His voice was calm and he pulled down on her wrists and it brought them closer together and then she stood up on her toes and kissed him gently on the lips.

"I really liked last night," She said this as she was taking a half step backward to look up at him in the innocent way all women do to a man they admire.

"Me too." He smiled at her and she couldn't help herself. Her arms were around his neck just like when he had opened the door last night and before either of them had time to think she kissed him with a real and true kiss and he felt it in his whole body.

He grabbed the small of her back and pulled her towards him kissing her deeply. They bumped into the bar and then turned and they were still kissing and then they bumped into a stool and it fell over. She pulled his hair a little to pull him away and said, "No, I can't, I won't… You're just a boy."

"Why?" Was she crying, he wondered?

"I can't, OK; I just can't."

"OK, OK, relax…OK?" She was crying and he felt awkward. Woman are the queerest things he thought as she broke away and he saw now that she had big wet tears in her eyes.

"You don't understand; you're just a boy; boys never understand."

"But…" and then there was no one for him to talk to. She ran across the room after her last statement and he heard her feet hit each of the 12 stairs and the sound of her flip-flops as she ran down the hall and her door opening and shutting quickly.

"Women!" he said to no one and reached down to pick up the barstool they had knocked over. Afterwards he walked around behind the bar to grab a beer from the fridge. Digging in his pocket he found the correct change and left it on top of the register for whenever she came back.

He stood in the place where she had stood all night and drank his beer quickly. In this heat you only had approximately 12 minutes to finish your beer before it got warm and too flat to enjoy. He opened a new beer and set it on top of his old circles on the bar and stood there waiting for the bartender to return.

Another girl and her friend came up the stairs and into the bar, they were nice girls but they weren't the type that would understand his condition. He sold them a beer and put the money on the register and then told them he had to go. At this point he didn't have time to explain anything.

Walking past them he went downstairs to find the bartender. When he got to the bartender's room she wasn't there. She didn't come back to the hostel that night and he left in the morning for home and they never saw each other again.

I KILLED A BLACK DOG

BY SEAN MICHAEL HAYES

Made in the USA
Lexington, KY
26 January 2015